Crowns & Tiaras

Crowns & Tiaras

Add a Little Sparkle, Glitter & Glamour to Every Day

Kerri Judd &
Danyel Montecinos

 LARK BOOKS

A Division of Sterling Publishing Co., Inc.
New York / London

A Red Lips 4 Courage Communications, Inc. book

www.redlips4courage.com

Eileen Cannon Paulin
President
Catherine Risling
Director of Editorial

Editor
Erika Kotite
Copy Editors
Laura Best
Catherine Risling
Book Designers
Meghan Farrington
Jocelyn Foye
Photographer
Denny Nelson
Photo Stylist
Sunday Hendrickson

Library of Congress
Cataloging Publication Data

Judd, Kerri, 1961-
Danyel Montecinos.
Crown & tiaras/ Kerri Judd & Danyel Montecinos. -- 1st ed.
    p. cm.
 Includes index.
 ISBN-13: 978-1-60059-097-9 (hc-plc with jacket : alk. paper)
 ISBN-10: 1-60059-097-7 (hc-plc with jacket : alk. paper)
 1. Crowns. 2. Tiaras. I. Montecinos, Danyel, 1968-
 II. Title.
TT171.J94 2007
745.5--dc22

10 9 8 7 6 5 4 3 2 1

First Edition

Published by Lark Books, A Division of
Sterling Publishing Co., Inc.
387 Park Avenue South, New York, NY 10016

Text © 2007, Kerri Judd and Danyel Montecinos
Photography © 2007, Red Lips 4 Courage Communications, Inc.

Distributed in Canada by Sterling Publishing,
c/o Canadian Manda Group, 165 Dufferin Street
Toronto, Ontario, Canada M6K 3H6

Distributed in the United Kingdom by GMC Distribution Services,
Castle Place, 166 High Street, Lewes, East Sussex, England BN7 1XU

Distributed in Australia by Capricorn Link (Australia) Pty Ltd.,
P.O. Box 704, Windsor, NSW 2756 Australia

If you have questions or comments about this book, please contact:
Lark Books
67 Broadway
Asheville, NC 28801
(828) 253-0467

Manufactured in China

ISBN 10: 1-60059-097-7
ISBN 13: 978-1-60059-097-9

For information about custom editions, special sales, premium and
corporate purchases, please contact Sterling Special Sales Department
at (800) 805-5489; or e-mail specialsales@sterlingpub.com.

"Because we hold our heads high, through triumph and adversity; because our hearts are full and our hands desire to create great beauty for others; because we deeply honor the gifts of our beloved friends and family and want to celebrate those gifts in an extraordinary way; that is why we create crowns."

—Kerri Judd & Danyel Montecinos

Contents

Introduction

There are thousands of unsung queens and princesses in our midst and it's time we did something about it. Crowning ourselves doesn't involve overthrowing any governments or storming Buckingham Palace—heavens, no, it's much simpler than that. Because in our own way each of us is royal, we must declare our queendom and create a crown that fits. This book will show you precisely how.

It used to be that only members of the monarchy and other special personages could wear a crown or tiara. Today, it's all about self-realized royalty. There's a new monarchy in charge, and you are part of the imperial reign. It's about time you crowned yourself or a special friend in the manner deserved, whether your blood runs blue, red, or a bright shade of purple.

So step, if you please, into the royal chambers of the most talented and esteemed artists and experience crowns that go way beyond the ordinary. These crowns and tiaras range from sparkling stunners to winsome whimsies, inspiring the beholder to make her own little masterpiece. Each crown makes a wonderful gift to treasure forever or commemorate a special day. Whatever the purpose, it's time to go from "unsung" to singing at the top of our lungs, "Long Live the Queen!"

Tidings from Kerri

If I ever won an award for Best Crown, you can be sure I would have at least one lady on my thank-you list: Glinda the Good Witch of the North. To her I owe my lifelong fascination with crowns and tiaras. The moment I saw her in "The Wizard of Oz" I dubbed her the most beautiful witch in the whole world—and I've been drawing elaborate crowns on the heads of princesses and queens, fairies and little girls, ever since.

Wearing a crown isn't a luxury, it's a necessity. It completes us. It's a girl thing. Put a little sparkle on my head and a song in my heart, and I'm good to go.

As someone who shamelessly treasures my childhood, I can hardly begin to tell you how I feel about crowns and tiaras, but in this book I'm going to give it my best shot. They've become a colossal part of my artistic expression and an extraordinary way of celebrating the lives and loves of the women who wear them.

After all, didn't you know that every woman is the queen of something? Her Royal Highness might rule as the queen of organization or reign supreme as the queen of bubble baths. Whatever queendom you reign over, put on your crown and by all means, wear it well.

Danyel's Royal Proclamation

When I was a child, every holiday my great-grandma Nelly gave each of her granddaughters a special box containing one or two pieces of her old costume jewelry. I played with the jewels for hours, turning my ordinary Barbie into Miss America with an earring crown and a bracelet sash. There was even a pastel tiara-shaped necklace I would turn upside down and balance on my own head like a crown.

These warm memories of the past are what spark my love of crowns, which I try to incorporate into my work every chance I get.

Crowns suggest great things, like royalty, victory, and success. They are made from precious things (or things cleverly fashioned from cool, inexpensive objects that only look precious), reflecting the priceless gifts we all have inside of us. The following pages will provide a journey of dazzling fantasy as we share some of our favorite artists' masterpieces with you.

What makes these head ornaments so compelling and alluring? Why are we drawn to them like moths to a flame? The answer is that it's the magic, the way you feel when you put on a crown or tiara. All of a sudden your shoulders go back and your head tilts high and proud. You are a queen, commanding the respect and attention you so amply deserve.

Just as the saying "There is a lid for every pot" goes, we feel there is a crown for every woman. Turn the page and let us help you find yours.

The Royal Workshop

*T*he modern crowns and tiaras of today's democracy are created in all shapes and sizes, composed of an almost infinite variety of papers, metals, trims, trinkets, and surprisingly ordinary household objects. So much of the fun of making these works of art is the high likelihood that at any given moment, you will stumble upon an object that will become the cornerstone of an original creation, celebrating the gifts and uniqueness of its recipient.

So while serendipity plays a big part in conjuring up a dazzling headpiece, the astute crown designer surrounds herself with the supplies that will be used again and again. As your crown-making avocation evolves, you will want to find a good place to work and a system for storing your tools and materials that works for you.

Places, Please

Start by getting some kind of drawer system; it can be an old dresser foraged from the garage or a set of nifty clear stacking plastic drawers. The important thing is that everything has its own place. Then, begin sorting. You can place all of your tools in one drawer; or, if the space is too small, separate your tools by function—for example, scissors, wire cutters, and paper punches.

The same goes for buttons and feathers. It's best to keep like colors together either by using plastic storage bags or smaller containers. (*Hint*: Don't throw out those jelly jars and empty prescription bottles; they are useful for keeping things separated and organized.)

Rhinestones and beads are more manageable if separated by color. Get a few bead containers, preferably the same size so they will stack on top of each other. Once supplies have a home, you will find that some things work better for you than others. Some artists prefer all of their containers to match in both size and color like a blank canvas so there is no confusion. Others get inspired by displaying each item in a wonderful little container—bowls and funky found shelves, old cabinets and apothecary jars. It's completely up to you. You are unique with your own ideas, so let your heart dictate what is right for you and have a great time setting up your creative sanctuary.

Paper stores well in a file drawer with hanging files that are labeled by color and pattern. Legal size is best so that you can thumb through them more quickly. If your paper is on rolls, consider thin, short curtain rods to hang them on.

The Essentials

Here we offer the fundamental ingredients for crowns and tiaras, and how they are used. With time and a few crowns under your belt, you will soon build your own list of essentials that may be quite different from this. That is, after all, what queens do.

Adhesives

Clear adhesive

Cyanoacrylates (liquid fast-drying adhesives) are great for adhering rhinestones to glass or metal. Remember that a little goes a long way. If the adhesive drips onto jewels, they will appear cloudy. Take a cotton swab dipped in jewelry or glass cleaner and rub the jewel until it sparkles again. Another option is dimensional adhesive that dries to a clear glass-like finish that's water-based and mixable. Use it to glue glitter, beads, glass, plastic, and vellum to paper; to adhere jewels to metal or porcelain; and spread evenly over artwork to give a raised, glass-like finish.

Double-stick tape

Look for the kind that is super tacky. Double-stick tape is usually applied by laying it on the project surface then peeling off the plastic to reveal the other sticky side. The Queens of Chaos among us love the fact that there is no sticky mess.

Epoxy

A strong, rubbery adhesive that dries with a shatter-resistant finish. Epoxies work well on metal-to-metal and metal-to-plastic projects as well as for adhering rhinestones.

Glitter glue

Commonly used for kids' crafts (always test first, as some brands will peel). Glitter glue designed for scrapbooking is user-friendly and adheres well.

Glue stick

Very convenient, good for adhering paper to paper. Look for brands that are permanent and acid-free.

Hot glue/glue gun

There are different strengths and temperatures of hot glue, but for the most part the kind you find at craft stores is fine. The greatest advantage of hot glue is that it dries quickly.

Mounting spray

Good for all-over coverage, mounting spray is also perfect for adhering glitter.

White glue/craft glue

Old-fashioned white glue is still a good choice, especially for adhering papers and fibrous trims. For best results, thin glue by mixing in a small amount of water.

Buttons

Buttons are so easy to work with and readily available, you'll be using them constantly. Stack them, string them like charms, treat them like jewels—the possibilities are endless. Make sure you remove buttons before discarding old shirts. Also, it is not beneath your dignity as queen to paw through bins of rummage sale shirts to find prize buttons.

Rhinestones

Rhinestones, hands down a favorite thing to use on crowns, spell glamour better than anything else. They are available in many different sizes, shapes, colors, and grades. They can be hand-cut and very expensive, but the machine-cut are beautiful as well.

You can buy rhinestones that have adhesive on the back or those adhered with a hot fix tool (when heated they stick to cloth and most types of paper). Another option is acrylic stones, which depending on their quality, are sometimes difficult to distinguish from the real thing.

Beads

Our advice: Amass as many beautiful beads as possible. Make sure you have a wide array of colors, shapes, and sizes as beads can either be strung onto wire or adhered directly to fabric, metal, plastic, or paper.

Dresdens

Nothing declares "Hail Victoria" better than a Dresden, the wonderful and versatile decorative trim that is used widely in holiday ornaments and crafts. Dresdens are die-cut, embossed paper covered in gold or silver foil. Both vintage and reproduction trims are available in a seemingly infinite variety of designs. Dresden trim can be used on crowns both for finishing (i.e. hiding wires and tape) and for lavish embellishment.

Metallic Thread

Delicate and magical, metallic threads have long been appreciated for the extra shimmer they add to jewelry making, embroidering, and now, crown making. They come in a large variety of colors and weights. Use metallic thread to cover bare wire, weaving two or more colors together for extra richness. It's also perfect for tying decorative tags or embellishments onto your crown.

Feathers

Use feathers for the tip of a party hat or to back a beautiful angel face for the focal point of an extraordinary holiday crown. Available in an array of colors.

Make It Shine
How to add extra sparkle to your crown jewels.

When gluing jewels to paper, use a dab of glitter gel and press the jewel into it. The result is an easy "frame" that surrounds your jewel with even more sparkle!

Instant Patina
Combine embossed wallpaper and a little paint for antique magic.

Here is a simple technique to achieve instant aging for your paper crowns. Using embossed wallpaper, apply spray paint in the color of your choice. Then apply a staining spray over the top and lightly wipe off the stain while it is still wet. Floral spray paints work well as they do not crack or peel.

Stand-Out Stones
Make your jewels really dazzle.

When using rhinestones, you can achieve a more finished look by adding a backing to them. Try mounting them in a bezel or some other prong setting (usually available where new rhinestones are sold); or set them on some wonderful buttons.

Glitter
Standard glitter

Standard glitter comes is many different colors and textures, from ultra fine to very coarse. In general, the finer the glitter the better the coverage. Coarser glitter is difficult to adhere.

German glass glitter

Crushed glass (which is very hard to find) is commonly referred to as vintage glass glitter. This glitter must be used with caution, as it can cut. The color also fades and tarnishes over time but it's the best thing to use if you are looking for vintage charm.

Mica

Another rare glitter, if you can call it glitter, mica is more like a pearlized flake that was used a lot in the 1950s. It can be difficult to find but well worth the search, since it will give a project that special charm from long ago.

Spray glitter

Comes in a can. Very subtle but nice to use for an all-over sparkle. Can also use it as an adhesive for loose glitter if you work fast and sprinkle fine glitter immediately after spraying before it has time to dry.

Fabrics

Always keep your eyes open for unique and unusual fabrics. Work with fabrics much like you do paper. Fabric can also be ruched (ruffled), pleated, or cut out and appliquéd. Experiment with fabric stiffener as well.

Paper

The sky is the limit here. Handmade paper, crinkle paper, crepe paper, wrapping paper, scrapbook paper, wallpaper, and even paper dolls are just a few of the options before you. Remember that some paper is too thin and delicate to hold up by itself. Give it some support by backing it with cardstock or posterboard. Adhere it with mounting spray and let it set a bit before cutting it to your desired shape.

Wallpaper is especially fun to use because of its firmness. It's flexible enough to shape and easy to cut, but it rarely needs backing. Embossed wallpaper such as Anaglypta is a wonderful choice for its texture and pattern (referred to as relief), and is perfect for painting. You can sometimes find it at home improvement stores or order it online.

Tinsel

Besides glitter, nothing makes the crown or tiara glimmer more beautifully than well-placed tinsel. Best results come from the vintage kind, with its nice bit of tarnished glamour. But using new tinsel means you will likely have more options at your disposal.

Angel hair tinsel

A very fine version of standard tinsel strands, angel hair tinsel is also slightly crinkled. It may be used for making nests or soft backgrounds on which to place Victorian scraps or other embellishments.

Crinkle wire

Although it's not exactly tinsel, this old-fashioned wire with its tiny zig-zag bends provides the same glittering effect.

Tinsel garland

One continuous string with short tufts of tinsel attached—great for winding around a crown base.

Tinsel wire

A smaller version of tinsel garland, tinsel wire comes in an array of colors.

Bezels

Bezels are the metal frames or disks into which jewels are set. There are flat-back bezels and prong bezels, which have a deeper cup.

Wire

Wire comes in many different gauges (weights); the higher the number, the thinner the wire. Most crown bases should be made with a 16-gauge wire; 19- or 22-gauges are ideal for the design. For fine beading, 34-gauge is just right; anything under 20-gauge starts to get a little too thick for beads and does not move easily enough for fine detail work.

Ribbon

We cannot rave enough about ribbon—it's an absolute essential among essentials for virtually every project. Always keep a lookout for beautiful print textures and colors—they just may be the inspiration you need. Remember to save scraps from the end of a roll and gifts you receive; these we refer to as tidbits, and you never know when you might need one. To remove wrinkles, touch them up with a hair flat iron.

Jewelry

Any kind of jewelry is great to have in your craft supplies—onesie earrings, broken chains, necklaces with missing stones, or pieces that have discolored too much to wear. These flaws do not matter when the jewelry is recycled for crowns, and in fact may add to its overall character and charm. To successfully disassemble a broken brooch, remove all of the remaining stones and place them in your jewel compartment. Remove the backing with a pair of wire cutters and spray or leaf the piece with gold or silver and use it for something else.

Tools of the Trade

With just a few tools, you can design truly majestic crowns. We start with a list of basic necessities, followed by our "luxury list" of tools that are wonderful to have and should be on any wish list.

Basic Tools

Needle-nose pliers

Needle-nose pliers make life easy for the crown maker. They can be used for many things, such as getting into small places, pinching things together, and manipulating curly wire into shapes. There are several different kinds of pliers: standard, flat surface (for fragile finishes), round-edge (to make small loops and "I" hooks), and curved nose.

Scissors

A woman cannot have too many pairs of shoes—or scissors. Keep several pairs on hand, including craft, paper, fabric, and decorative-edge scissors and pinking shears.

Wire cutters

Wire cutters are an absolute necessity when working with wire. Never use your scissors to cut wire or the blades will chip. Any wire cutters are fine for most crown work.

Useful Extras

As you spend more time working on regal creations, start adding some of these little helpers. Their usefulness will make you want to whistle while you work.

Cotton swabs For cleaning up glue residue or to gently feather paint or glitter.

Floral tape For covering wire to give your crown or tiara base a smooth, workable surface for adding embellishments.

Nail file For dulling a sharp edge after a shank or pin backing is broken off.

Rhinestone grabber A metal syringe-looking tube that picks up individual rhinestones and places them exactly where you want. Another option is a toothpick with a small amount of beeswax on the tip.

Shank nippers For removing the shanks off button backs.

Tongue depressors, popsicle sticks, wooden matchsticks Use to back paper or fabric for support.

Tweezers For grabbing tiny beads or buttons.

Estate Secrets

Begin, Already
Don't be afraid to start, or you'll never finish.

There is no right or wrong way to start a project. Once you have decided what you are using for a base, you may have a technique that works best for you, whether it be starting with a background and building to the foreground, or starting in the center and embellishing your way around the sides. The final results is all that matters.

Collage Degree
Here's a crash course in collaging your crowns.

To collage a crown, start with an interesting background, such as a map, some sheet music, old floral wallpaper, or vintage book pages. Layer images on top of one another with an adhesive that seals, glues, and finishes. Use papers of various colors, textures, and sizes—you can cut them with decorative-edge scissors, tear them, twist them, or crinkle them and then straighten them out.

Shopping Pointers

When building your royal workshop there are a few additional strategies to keep in mind in order to better chart your course.

First, understand that shopping for crown supplies is fun. And sometimes that is *all* it is. Your net may frequently come up empty, and you will seldom find everything you need in one stop. Shopping trips should be made periodically to slowly build up each crown project—pieces are then tucked away into a shoebox, cubby, or plastic sealable bag and stored until everything is ready.

While shopping, let your vision be changed or further encouraged by even a tiny embellishment. A shiny antique earring can inspire an amazing princess tiara, while old skeleton keys excite a crown. Crowns do not always originate the same way.

It's not always an object that sparks a crown—sometimes it's a color or a group of colors that launches an idea. Whimsical objects you see while flipping through a catalog or magazine, or a bouquet that catches your eye as you pass a floral shop, can inspire a crown or tiara.

Some crown makers bring along a small sketchbook in their purse to capture visions before they fade. But don't be surprised if you find yourself rushing home to get started.

The Crown Jewels

Empress *of* Impress

*I*n nature, females are often quite plain compared to their male counterparts. Think peahen and peacock. With apologies to Mother Nature, that biological fact is strictly for the birds.

Therefore, keeping in mind all of the fabulous fashionistas in your life, a crown created with the luscious colors of the peacock is the perfect finishing touch for stylish regalia.

Waking from a dream where plumes and colors of the peacock bedecked a fireplace mantel, the artist turned that vision into reality with this flashy and oh-so-sumptuous peacock crown.

The bold, bright colors of this crown are like a New Orleans party waiting to happen. Wear it and start shaking those tail feathers.

22

Make Your Own
{empress of impress}

Directives

1. Beginning with a 15"-square piece of embossed wallpaper, draw a pattern the shape of a large piece of pie. Cut paper in this shape. Spray paint it gold, and form a cone shape, overlapping edges and securing with hot-glue gun.

2. Cut out base from coordinating embossed wallpaper; adhere to front of cone.

3. Adhere vintage lace atop base and wire-edge ribbon at bottom of base.

4. Along with a few holiday tree ornaments that happen to be precisely the right accessories, embellish the cone with tinsel trim, rhinestones, and a sprinkling of sequins using craft glue.

5. In great pomp and triumph, a jeweled medallion with feathers at front center and the iconic peacock himself perched on a bed of tinsel are the top notes in this regal masterpiece.

6. To make sure the Empress of Impress doesn't lose her head, affix some ribbon streamers on each side.

" There can only be one peacock in a relationship."
—Darren Calkins

Tools & Adhesives

- craft glue
- fabric scissors
- hot-glue gun
- paper scissors
- ruler

Royal Trimmings

- embossed wallpaper, 2
- gimp trim
- gold spray paint
- holiday ball ornaments
- jeweled medallions
- peacock feathers
- peacock ornament
- rhinestones
- sequins
- tinsel trim
- wire-edge ribbon, 2

Queen of the Not-So-Broken Heart

It happens to the best of us—a breakup, a Dear Jane letter, or the wretched "D" word. To be Queen of the Not-So-Broken Heart is to acknowledge a bruised heart with a tiara even a Tsarina would envy. Dozens of shimmering garnets are like tiny drops of a broken heart's blood, set against a delightfully rich gold leaf background.

Creating this piece can take time but the end result is certainly worth it. A few yards of gold craft wire are bent into a pleasing tiara form. A couple of coats of sizing glue are applied, followed by plenty of gold leaf bits.

Small clusters of rough-cut garnets and tiny freshwater pearls are twisted on with gold wire, with a few vintage rhinestones added here and there for good measure. The paper flowers sprinkled about are punched out of an old business card, and then accented with polished diamond chips and more garnets within the centers.

There is no better way to help a friend start a new chapter in her life than to proclaim her Queen and hand her a tiara dripping in gold, diamonds, and garnets. After all, her heart may be broken but her flair and sense of fun are not.

Make Your Own

{queen of the not-so-broken heart}

Directives

1. Cut 12" piece of 22-gauge craft wire. Curl ends into half circle and unravel 24" length of 19-gauge craft wire. Leaving it on the roll, twist half the length onto crown base to secure, then twist around one-third of base and begin forming 3"-tall daisy-shaped floret. At end of floret, twist wire back onto tiara base to the center halfway mark.

2. Twist second 4"-tall floret in center of base. At end of floret twist onto base again, continue around, and at ⅓" mark, again twist a third 3"-tall floret. Finish twisting wire along remaining section of tiara base; cut off.

3. Apply thick coat of gold leaf sizing; let dry to a light tack. With your index finger and thumb, pinch on gold leaf, applying as much as desired. Cut 6" lengths of 22-gauge wire and slide on three or four garnets to form clusters; twist ends closed. Do the same with pearls, making a few dozen and twisting all over tiara.

4. Cut three 8" lengths of crepe paper. Cut in half lengthwise; sew gathering stitch along fold side. Tug gently and gather into a circle. Seal with dab of glue.

5. Cut out three "cameos" from historical portraits; decoupage onto cardstock. Cut out and adhere to center of crepe paper circle with glue. Adhere each crepe paper floret to center of wire florets on crown. Hold in place with small clamps until dry. Glue jewelry remnants and more garnets around cameo to accent. Adhere book text to cardstock. Cut out three small semi-circles and roll into small cone-shaped hats. Accent with tiny triangles of paper and glue onto tops of paper cameos.

6. Using flower paper punch, punch out florets from business cards. Adhere to crown and glue gems into center. Make tiny bow out of a small bit of embroidery thread and glue to center cameo.

Tools & Adhesives

- craft glue
- decoupage medium
- flower paper punch
- foam brush
- gold leaf sizing glue
- needle and thread
- paper scissors
- pliers
- small clamps, 3
- wire cutters

Royal Trimmings

- 19-gauge craft wire
- 22-gauge brass wire
- beige crepe paper streamer
- book text
- business cards
- cardstock
- freshwater pearls
- garnets
- gold leaf
- historical portraits, 3
- jewelry remnants
- pink embroidery thread
- vintage rhinestones

Estate Secrets

Saving for a Rainy Day

Find a cure for heartbreak with gathering tips.

• Save all the leftover gold leaf crumbs from other projects; they work perfectly on this project as you only need small bits and pieces.

• Always save pretty business cards you collect, they come in handy with a flower punch. Everything looks brighter with little paper flowers all over!

• Never pass up old gemstone necklaces or bracelets at thrift stores and tag sales. Break them apart and use them on your projects. They're the best way to get real luxe on the cheap.

• Never, never throw away even the smallest bit of paper; you never know what it might become.

" A girl should be two things: classy and fabulous."

— Coco Chanel

Ice Princess

The Snow Queen. Queen Frosting. Snowflake Fairy. Why do so many of the storybook creatures who enthralled us as children find ice and snow worthy of sovereign rule? Snow is cold, wet, and really quite odious when it buries your car or freezes your pipes. And yet, consider the miracle of the stuff, created from billions upon billions of tiny snowflakes, each one a geometric miracle of precision and symmetry—God's lace, gentle as a kiss and strong as the wind. Wouldn't it really be something to be ruler of this winter wonderland?

To rule, however, one needs a tiara that heralds the true fantasy and mystery of the world when it is blanketed in crystals of white. Here it all starts with a child's plastic beaded tiara, stripped down to its bare bones. A large, iridescent snowflake is the crown jewel for this icy confection. Some silver tinsel is added around the bottom along with a rhinestone studded ribbon. Dangling in the openings of the crown are some clear, sparkling gems.

This tiara will make any woman pick it up and, with her face illuminated by its shimmer, announce, "Look, I am the Snow Queen." That's what wearing a tiara is all about.

Make Your Own
{ice princess}

Directives

1. Begin with a plastic tiara as the base. If the plastic is too shiny, you can antique it with a floral spray stain or wood stain. If you spray the plastic, be sure it is completely dry before continuing.

2. On this tiara, it's all about the snowflakes. Place your large snowflake ornament in the center of the tiara and adhere with hot glue. Adhere diamond button to center of snowflake. Scatter the other smaller snowflakes around in a pleasing pattern and glue in place.

3. Tuck wired rhinestones behind large snowflake and hot glue in place. Place extra rhinestones on snowflakes using craft glue. Glue silver leaves behind large snowflakes.

4. Wire chandelier pendants with 26-gauge wire and affix to the various openings in the tiara front.

5. Wind tinsel garland around base of tiara and adhere with hot glue. Place rhinestone trim on top of tinsel and glue in place. Finish inside of tiara by gluing trim to cover base.

Tools & Adhesives

- craft glue
- hot-glue gun
- rhinestone grabber
- shank nippers
- wire cutters

Royal Trimmings

- 1 large, 4 small frosted snow-flake ornaments
- 26-gauge wire
- chandelier pendants
- diamond button
- grosgrain ribbon
- plastic beaded tiara
- rhinestone trim
- rhinestones
- silver glittered leaves
- tinsel garland
- wired rhinestones

Estate Secrets

Button Hunting

Crown makers have an endless fascination
with these wonderful fasteners.

While the Amish may view buttons as a worldly vanity, for most people from the 19th century on, buttons were nothing less than jewelry for clothes. Exquisite gem-encrusted buttons, silver buttons embossed with dogs or sailboats, and gleaming pearl buttons are all highly coveted by collectors today.

One way to find great buttons for your crown project is to explore thrift stores and garage sales. There you'll find old dresses and coats that often have amazing buttons sewn on them. Buy the piece at very little expense and you may end up with buttons worth many times that amount.

"If you want a happy ending, that depends, of course, on where you stop your story."

— Orson Welles

{crown}

Woodland Fairy

*I*n this overheated, pasteurized, homogenized world, women have very few chances to exercise their wild side.

One look at this soft, crinkle paper crown, with its dreamlike vista of woodland children marching around its circumference, and the words of Henry Thoreau come wonderfully to mind: "The indescribable innocence and beneficence of Nature—of sun and wind and rain, of summer and winter—such health, such cheer, they afford forever!"

So, when it's hard to see the forest for the buildings and board meetings, just step away from the Blackberry, don the Woodland Fairy crown, and go foraging for some real, unplugged blackberries.

Make Your Own
{woodland fairy}

Directives

1. Start with a posterboard base about 20" x 9" and cover with pink paper using craft glue. Line with an equal piece of white felt. Trim top into scallops or other decorative design. Glue short ends together with hot glue to create a crown. Take a wide strip of white tissue paper (about 5") and fold it in half, and then create fringe with scissors. Glue this on inside top of crown with craft glue, following the curves of the design.

2. Assemble your "adopted family" of vintage children photos and make copies of them on matte photo paper, reducing and enlarging so they are same size. Glue them onto cardstock with craft glue, and then cut them out.

3. Dress children in outfits made of felt, cotton batting, old lace, and vintage trims, attaching with hot glue; adhere children around the crown with hot glue. Tuck small craft branches behind children so that ends are hidden; glue in place using hot glue. Finish bottom of crown by adhering felt trim with pom-poms using hot glue.

Tools & Adhesives
- craft glue
- craft scissors
- decorative-edge scissors
- fabric scissors
- hot-glue gun

Royal Trimmings
- cotton batting
- craft branches
- felt trim with small pompoms
- matte photo paper
- pink art or handmade paper
- posterboard
- vintage children's photos
- vintage lace, trim
- white felt
- white tissue paper

Her Holiness of Matrimony

Remembering the days of poodle skirts and diners with fancy neon signs, one can easily wax nostalgic for the kitschy glamour of the 1950s. Those were the days when martinis were mixed in pitchers, pink flamingoes ornamented the lawns, and the bride still tucked sprigs of orange blossoms into her veil.

Perhaps the wonderful vintage sequined letters that dress this playful crown once glinted on the costumes of tiny tap dancers who dreamed they'd be the next Shirley Temple.

While Js might stand for "Joy" or "Jubilee," be creative with whichever letter you chance to find. It really goes to show that while the Anniversary Queen is justifiably proud of her happy married life and knows that time is fleeting, she hasn't stopped dancing.

Make Your Own
{her holiness of matrimony}

Directives

1. The plastic ring used for base of crown can be a wide embroidery hoop, or a large plastic ring used for macrame projects. Paint ring with silver spray paint.

2. Paint beaded trim with silver spray paint. Antique with floral and wood stains; let dry. Adhere trim to inside of base with hot glue.

3. Cut one 3" wire for each sequin letter. Adhere wire to back of each letter with hot glue. Attach each letter to base using epoxy to hold the bottom of each wire.

4. Hot glue silver beaded trim to outside of base. Crinkle vintage silver thread tinsel and glue to top of base with hot glue.

Tools & Adhesives
- epoxy
- hot-glue gun
- wire cutters

Royal Trimmings
- 20-gauge wire
- beaded trim, 1" wide, enough for inside and outside of base
- floral spray stain
- plastic ring, large enough to fit around head
- silver spray paint
- vintage sequined letters
- vintage silver thread tinsel
- wood spray stain

"Our wedding was many years ago. The celebration continues to this day"

— Gene Perret

Princess of Happily Ever After

When Cinderella danced with the Prince in her size 5 shoes, she couldn't have been more than 17 years old. Of course, that's why it's called a fairy tale. For the more mature princess, who cannot depend on a fairy godmother to transform her clothes, pets, and vegetable garden, a magical crown like this might do the trick.

Whether she is hoping for romance to come into her life or simply beginning a new chapter in a new house or a new career, the Princess of Happily Ever After needs a crown announcing that it's never too late to find your happy ending.

Make Your Own
{princess of happily ever after}

Directives

1. Begin with embossed wallpaper base shaped into a cone-shaped hat; hot glue edges together. Cut brim from different embossed wallpaper pieces. Attach cone to inside of brim with hot glue.

2. Attach silk ribbons on each side of cone to keep crown secure on Her Ladyship's head. Attach decorative trim to outside of brim with hot glue. Attach gimp trim over decorative trim with hot glue.

3. Adhere swirls of sequin trim all over cone with hot glue.

4. Gather a few pale blue and cream feathers and tape together. Keep adding until you get desired look.

5. String beads and crystals onto medium-firm wire. Fold ends to secure. Add to feather bouquet with tape. When finished, give bouquet a clean cut at the bottom. Nip an opening on top of cone and fit bouquet in place with hot glue.

6. Add rhinestones, adhering with epoxy. Add cameo brooch, watch face, and any other sparkle you please.

Tools & Adhesives

- epoxy
- hot-glue gun
- ruler
- scissors
- silver spray paint
- tape: cellophane, floral
- wire cutters

Royal Trimmings

- beads
- cameo brooch
- crystals
- decorative trim
- embossed wallpaper, 2 types
- feathers: cream, pale blue
- gimp trim
- ribbon
- sequin trim
- watch face
- wire

*M*ost people get nice cards of congratulations upon graduating from college or university but surely a dazzling tiara better reflects this amazing accomplishment. Besides, what could be less attractive on a well-coiffed head than a plain old mortarboard?

The recipient of this quick and easy tiara had worked a day job while studying nights. She richly earned her title, Queen of Co-Eds. After the graduation ceremony, she wore her tiara proudly out to celebrate and received a great deal of attention—and even garnered a free round of drinks from the next table over. In short, the tiara made a momentous event much more festive and fun.

Word has it that the Queen keeps her tiara on the lampshade next to her bed as a simple reminder of her great achievement. It also reminds her that happily, there will be no more late-night studying, and only success is ahead.

Make Your Own
{matriculating majesty}

Directives

1. Starting with a thin plastic headband, wrap with ½" paper strips cut from a page of an old book and secure ends with glue (see tiara instructions, page 114).

2. Adhere crown-shaped Dresden to front.

3. Clip a sparkling earring onto front center of tiara.

4. Wrap gold tinsel around earring, weaving around stones.

Tools & Adhesives

- paper scissors
- water-based dimensional adhesive

Royal Trimmings

- clip-on vintage earring
- gold Dresden
- gold tinsel
- old book page
- thin plastic headband

Heiress to the Throne

*B*elow the rooms of Buckingham Palace lies the underground treasury of the Windsor family's multi-billion-dollar fortune—exquisite gifts of jewelry, silver, artwork, and china given to the monarchy. Each little prince and princess who comes along becomes an enviable heir to the family jewels.

The desire to pass something down to future generations runs strong in every heart, blueblood or not.

For a commoner, raiding Grandmother's costume jewelry box brought forth an impressive array of bejeweled pieces that were torn apart, remixed, and reused for a young princess. Additional beads and rhinestones were added, strung onto wire and shaped into a crown. Dangling inside the finial is a vintage earring.

Make Your Own
{heiress to the throne}

Directives

1. Using needle-nose pliers, take vintage jewelry pieces apart.

2. Cut two pieces of 22-gauge florist's wire at least 4" long. String beads on both wires in desired pattern for 4". Repeat to make five more pieces. You can alter the pattern, but making matching pairs will give crown symmetry. After 4", split wires and string individually for 1½". Bring wires together again with rhinestone bead. Repeat until wires are long enough to be brought together at top of crown.

3. Create base in same way, using two strands of 20-gauge wire long enough to fit on top of head. Wrap wire ends together to create circle. Wire shoe clip to base.

4. Attach previously made strands to base by wrapping wire ends around base tightly. After all side pieces are attached, join together in center at top of crown. String several additional short wires pieces to decorate top of crown.

5. Add any additional pieces of jewelry to crown with wire. Hang earring from center by wrapping it to top of crown with 22-gauge wire. Fill in spaces as desired with silver crinkle wire.

Tools & Adhesives

- needle-nose pliers
- thick craft wire

Royal Trimmings

- 22-, 20-gauge florist's wire
- beads, rhinestones
- silver bullion
- silver crinkle wire
- vintage beaded necklaces, earrings, shoe clip

" Their virtues lived in their children. The family changed its persons but not its manners, and they continued a blessing to the world from generation to generation."

—The History of the Countess of Dellwyn, by Sarah Flemming

Provençale Princess

The joy in making and wearing crowns is that they so beautifully embody secret wishes and dreams. Whether these dreams truly become a reality or not doesn't matter so much; what really matters is that the dreams are manifest in works of art, allowing the dreamer to derive even more satisfaction from holding them close.

Envision the "dream house in Provence." Who hasn't had this dream of being the lady of the country manor house from time to time? Nothing fancy, of course—just an old stone place in the south of France, where even the most functional, rustic things seem to have a fabulous style and simple beauty. Delving deeper into this fantasy, picture a kitchen garden and a hen house filled with fresh eggs.

Don't worry about the tarnish, cracks, or chips on the elements used to make your French Farmhouse Dream crown. In France, real beauty is never about perfection; maybe that's why we love the place so much.

"What a thing it is to lie here all day in the fine breeze, with pine needles dropping on one, only to return to the hotel at night so hungry that the dinner, however homely, is a fête and the menu finer reading than the best poetry in all the world!"

-Willa Cather, in southern France 1902

Make Your Own
{provençale princess}

Directives

1. Remove mirror from mirror trim; set aside.

2. Cut large piece of chicken wire slightly longer than length of mirror trim. Using wire cutters, clip open bottom edge of chicken wire. Use edges of chicken wire to attach decorative trim (which already has holes in it from where it was attached to mirror).

3. Cut shape of chicken wire into pleasing crown shape. Lightly spray rust paint spots on chicken wire to lend aged appearance.

4. Attach second chicken wire piece to inside of base. Tuck velvet material into base, pulling tufts through to front. Hot glue velvet from underneath crown.

5. Weave vintage tinsel in and out of chicken wire at base and then attach vintage jewelry and glittered cardboard stars to chicken wire using craft wire.

6. Attach silver foil leaves to highlight shape of chicken wire with hot glue.

7. Embellish with old jewelry bits, trims, and beaded tassel as desired.

Tools & Adhesives

- hot-glue gun
- wire cutters

Royal Trimmings

- beaded tassle
- bullion
- cardboard stars
- chicken wire
- clear, silver, teal German glass glitter
- craft wire
- decorative paper
- old jewelry bits
- old vanity mirror trim
- rust spray paint
- silver foil leaves
- tinsel trim
- vintage orange fabric
- vintage tinsel

Estate Secrets

Playing Chicken

Chicken wire makes a charmingly rustic statement.

There is more to good ol' chicken wire than meets the eye. For example, did you know that it comes in many sizes and weights? For a delicate country touch on a crown project, opt for something on the smaller size and don't forget to wear your gloves. In fact, long-length rose gloves are best because they protect the arms, too.

Don't Call it Junk

Take a second look at damaged merchandise.

Once you start collecting pieces for crown making, you will completely lose your fastidiousness. Damaged and broken jewelry lying at the bottom of the clearance bin is just right for a weathered tiara or as forage for rhinestones. Remember that it is much easier to use something old than to try and make something new look old.

Princess of the Sea

The allure of the sea is strong in the human heart. Perhaps it's the steady beat of the waves that makes a heavy heart calm and a happy heart leap for joy. Little wonder, then, that so many lucky newlyweds head to a tropical paradise before launching into marital realities of a shared bathroom and joint tax returns.

The Princess of the Sea tiara, made with radiating medallions and stars of gleaming seashells, would make a beautiful wedding present for the bride planning a seaside honeymoon. Her tiara not only highlights her beauty but also pays lasting tribute to the magical place she plans to visit.

For the centerpiece, a design of shells was arranged, dusted with fine glass glitter, and adhered with a hot-glue gun onto star-shaped silver cardstock.

With a tiara that any self-respecting mermaid would envy, a woman is sure to master the deep blue sea that is called matrimony.

Make Your Own
{princess of the sea}

Directives

1. Cut two ¾"-wide strips of paper the length needed to cover the headband. Hot glue one strip to inside of headband. Hot glue other strip of paper to outside of headband.

2. To create central medallion for tiara: Cut large circle of silver cardstock with craft punch or using a template. Hot glue shells in desired pattern on oval and dust entire surface with glass glitter before hot glue has cooled: shake off excess glitter.

3. To create sides for tiara: Cut two sweeping triangles from cardstock. Coat front and back of pieces with craft glue and cover with silver glass glitter. Attach triangles to inside of headband with hot glue.

4. To create rosettes, stars, or flowers for front of crown: Choose shells of similar size and color to ensure symmetry. Hot glue shells in desired patterns on triangular pieces or smaller cardstock circles, ovals, or stars, dusting each with glass glitter before the hot glue has cooled.

5. Take center medallion and hot glue needle to back (the pointed tip should be in the center of the oval and extend down). Hot glue needle end to front of headband.

6. Using the craft wire, make a circle larger than the center medallion. Hot glue small shells to wire. Hot glue wire to triangle cardstock pieces.

7. Hot glue smaller shell rosettes and shell flowers to edges of medallion and headband as desired. As each piece is adhered, dust with glass glitter before hot glue cools. Add shells in pairs to fill in empty spaces on each side of tiara, remembering to dust each with glitter. Coat smaller blank spots of headband and exposed needle with craft glue, then coat with glass glitter.

8. Finish by making sure all inside cardstock parts of crown are covered with silver glitter.

Tools & Adhesives

- 3" heavy-duty sewing needle
- hot-glue gun
- paper scissors
- white craft glue

Royal Trimmings

- ½"-wide flexible plastic headband
- assorted oval and circle paper punches or templates
- assorted small and medium size shells
- fine silver glass glitter
- heavy-gauge craft wire
- paper strips
- silver cardstock at least 20" long

Countess of Confections

*I*t's a sad truth universally acknowledged that cinnamon buns, chocolate truffles, and New York cheesecake go right to the hips. But in the realm of magical kingdoms, glittering confectionary treats are meant to go nowhere but atop the head of deserving royalty.

Presenting the Countess of Confections crown. Literally bursting with lifelike candy, cookies, and chocolate-covered pretzels, this mouthwatering masterpiece is destined for that amazing friend who would do anything for you. She has picked up your kids after soccer practice, helped you plan a surprise party, baked you a cake on your birthday, and walked your dog when you were working late—all with a sweet smile and a glad heart.

For all the wonderful things she does, she truly deserves this crown. Her generosity sparkles like the glitter sugar that tops the truffles, cookies, and gumdrops.

Queen of Confectionary Delights

Make Your Own
{countess of confections}

Directives

1. Starting with a plastic headband for the base, glue on desired shape cut from decorative paper and reinforced with posterboard. Using glitter adhesive, cover with teal German glass glitter.

2. Adhere leaves, petals, and ribbon with epoxy and hot glue.

3. Embellish candies with different colors of German glass glitter—teal, sea green, pink, and fuchsia—and adhere to crown base with wire and epoxy. Adhere millinery fruits with wire and epoxy.

4. The image of the little girl holding the cake is a combination of three different images. All images were combined and resized using a computer and image-manipulation program.

5. Add ribbon streamers on each side of crown and title of your choice using hot glue.

"She has all the royal markings of a queen."
—King Henry VIII, by William Shakespeare

Tools & Adhesives
- computer and printer
- craft scissors
- epoxy
- glitter adhesive
- hot-glue gun

Royal Trimmings
- candy picks/ornaments
- decorative paper
- fuchsia, pink, sea green, teal German glass glitter
- millinery leaves, petals, fruit
- plastic headband
- posterboard
- ribbon
- vintage images of butterfly wings, cake, little girl
- wire

rowns and tiaras are gorgeous and all, but did you know they can be eco-friendly? All of those one-sie earrings taking up space in your jewelry box are the perfect salvage material for a regal rags-to-riches tiara.

This tiara's poise and petite elegance belies the fact that it celebrates the woman who recognizes the true beauty in castoffs and is obsessed with giving old things a second chance.

All the bits and baubles used for this tiara were from broken, unwanted jewelry. Each piece was revived with a little tender loving care, also known as ordinary jewelry cleaner. A little polishing and replacing of rhinestones can almost always bring jewels to life.

This tiara feels both unique and humble, almost commanding the Salvage Regina to "Keep me, wear me, take me out!"

Make Your Own
{salvage regina}

Directives

1. Using strong-hold glue, secure brooch in center of tiara base.

2. Using epoxy, glue jewelry backs and pressed-metal findings onto tiara to fill in background.

3. Starting in the center, build tiara with symmetrical jewelry. Find matching pieces (one for each side) and work your way to back of base. Place one or two jewels on top of the centerpiece. Adhere all pieces with strong-hold glue. Add button on each side using epoxy.

Tools & Adhesives
- epoxy
- strong–hold glue

Royal Trimmings
- metal or plastic tiara
- rhinestone brooches, buttons, earrings
- various jewelry pieces

{crown}

Queen of the May

Remember being a little girl and fantasizing about prancing around a maypole wearing the most amazing muslin dress with long sashes? That little girl is still somewhere inside, obscured perhaps by grown-up obligations and inhibitions. Promise, then, that the next time you wake up to a glorious spring day your fancy won't turn to thoughts of laundry to be done, but rather to fanciful papers, pompoms, and glitter. Instead of spring cleaning, it's time for Spring Queening.

Spring is all about hope and renewal, when the feeling of dew on bare feet evokes a momentary glimmer of how it felt to be a happy child. The Queen of the May assumes a special role in ensuring that an age-old tradition of welcoming springtime never ends.

Make Your Own
{queen of the may}

Directives

1. To create base of crown: Adhere decorative paper to 24" x 8" piece of poster-board using mounting adhesive. Trim top with decorative-edge scissors.

2. Apply velvet ribbon and pompom fringe to base of crown with craft glue. Attach velvet flowers to top of crown by taping on back.

3. Cover stems with small decorative cutouts (from endpapers or other scraps on hand). Create small florets by winding French wire ribbon around itself and securing centers with needle and thread. Glue rosettes to front of crown with craft glue; glue vintage buttons to center.

4. Bring edges of crown together and secure with double-stick tape. For more stability, add paper clips and cover them with small decorative paper cutouts.

Tools & Adhesives

- craft glue
- decorative-edge scissors
- mounting adhesive
- needle and thread
- paper clips
- paper scissors
- ruler
- tacky double-stick tape

Royal Trimmings

- decorative papers
- French wire ribbon
- pompom fringe
- posterboard
- velvet leaves
- velvet ribbon
- vintage buttons

Her Grace
of the
Garden

How does *your* garden grow? If roses make you sing or sweet peas make you swoon, you are officially mistress of your backyard kingdom. A woman's green thumb should be celebrated with a crown that reflects the tangled, fragrant, earthy paradise that is a garden.

This piece is a far cry from the old straw hat you may normally wear while digging in the dirt. Inspired by the works of Faberge as well as a beautiful garden trellis from *The Chronicles of Narnia*, curved bands suggest a rustic arbor. Each band is swathed in "moss" that is actually remnants of a tattered French ball gown, peppered with black pearls, garnets, pink tourmalines, and peridots. The base is constructed from an ordinary hanger covered in "moss" and old crepe paper.

Capturing the joy of looking close and seeing tiny buds emerge on a cold February afternoon, the floral details on this crown are too entrancing to ignore. Tiny blossoms made with micro collage are decoupaged onto cardstock, the petals are curled back, and a tiny golden freshwater pearl is adhered to each center.

As for Sweet Pea, the whimsical White Knight dangling in the middle, various black-and-white elements from old books are collaged together to create this delightful little spirit. While nothing takes the place of real flowers and dirt under your fingernails, a fantastical, frivolous crown for the Queen of the Sweet Peas makes every day in the garden a royal event.

Make Your Own
{her grace of the garden}

Directives

1. Twist one wire hanger into a circle form to create base. Fashion remaining hangers into crown arms. Connect arms to base by bending ends onto circle form; pinch closed with pliers.

2. Cut several 20" strips of crepe paper. Fold in half lengthwise and cover wire structure by winding crepe paper strips around in same fashion as wrapping floral tape on a stem. Cover entire crown, sealing ends with craft glue.

3. Cut several 6" lengths of 22-gauge wire. Fold in half and slide on bead, pearl, or several gemstones of your choice and twist remaining wire closed. Twist each one randomly around crown.

4. To make flower blossoms: Create your own collage on 8" x 10" sheet of blank white paper. Reduce on photocopier to 25 percent. Cut out micro-collage and adhere to cardstock with decoupage medium.

5. Working on a sheet of wax paper, punch out several dozen cardstock circles with hole punch. (Two needed for each blossom.) Cut out five teardrop-shaped petals for each flower. Place drop of craft glue on top of cardstock circle then lay in each petal; let dry. Gather outer edges of circle together and twist wire around bottom to make flower shape and stem; wire flower to crown. Repeat as many times as you like.

6. Tear several 12" lengths of lace and entwine over arms and base of crown, adding drops of glue here and there to secure.

7. Cut two ½" x 12" strips of velvet and wind around base of crown, again securing in spots with craft glue. Adhere crystals all over lace to further embellish. Add jewelry remnants as final accent.

8. Stamp whimsical image onto blank white paper with black ink and enlarge on photocopier 50 percent. Adhere image to cardstock with decoupage medium; cut out and glue under crown.

Tools & Adhesives

- craft glue
- decoupage medium
- fanciful rubber stamp
- hole punch
- paintbrush
- photocopier
- pliers
- wire cutters
- wire hangers, 3

Royal Trimmings

- 22-gauge wire
- assorted pearls, gems, crystals
- beige crepe paper streamer
- black ink
- blank white paper
- cardstock
- collage papers
- jewelry remnants
- velvet fabric or ribbon
- vintage lace
- wax paper

Tiny Art

Estate Secrets

Micro collage produces masterpieces of diminutive proportions.

Inspired by ancient mosaic floor design, micro collage is essentially cutting up tiny images to form an entirely new design. Take your favorite small pictures (from holiday tags, business cards, gift wrap, etc.) and reduce them even smaller on a color copier. Cut them up and reassemble them into a pleasing, entirely original piece. It shouldn't be more than 1½" in diameter. But wait Alice, we haven't stopped shrinking yet. Take the new design and reduce it one or two more times on a color copier. *Now*, you are ready to create tiny wonders for your crown projects.

{crown}

Crown Royale

*I*f you asked a child to draw a crown, it would likely be shaped like the one shown here. After all, children know very well what true royalty is—stately, worthy, dignified, and lavish. The colors of a true Crown Royale are jewel tones; the metal, of course, must be pure gold. There are certain rules to follow when you are crowning a true blue-blood.

It all begins with a small gold crown—religious websites carry these in small and full sizes. Most of the pieces on this crown came from old brooches, bracelets, and even miscellaneous clothing.

Since true blue-bloods are a bit scarce these days, consider a Crown Royale for someone who continually shows the makings of an imperial leader: compassion for her fellow citizens; the ability to make big decisions without fuss; and of course, someone who would look absolutely fabulous in a full-length royal cloak.

Make Your Own
{crown royale}

Directives

1. Starting with a gold crown base, cut off hanger. (***Hint***: You might find tree ornaments that work well or check stores or websites that sell crowns for religious statues.) Using epoxy, adhere a strand of rhinestones or old necklace or bracelet around the base of the crown, using clothespins to hold in place as adhesive sets.

2. Choose a spectacular jewel for the front center and adhere in place with strong-hold glue gel.

3. From there, work your way up and down the center of the crown, adding embellishments as you see fit. This is a perfect opportunity to use a lone earring, a broken bracelet, or bits of a necklace, filling in blank areas with rhinestones. Keep some sort of pattern consistent on all sides of the crown. Choose a fabulous piece as the crowning glory. (***Hint***: Strong-hold glue gel is best for glass stones and epoxy works best on larger pieces and acrylic stones.)

Tools & Adhesives
- clothespins
- epoxy
- strong-hold glue gel
- wire cutters

Royal Trimmings
- acrylic jewels
- bracelets
- brooches
- earrings
- gold crown base
- rhinestones

Queen of Extreme

Norma Shearer fans will surely re-member her in the 1938 movie, *Marie Antoinette*. In one scene she wore an unforgettable head ornament consisting of an ornate gilded birdcage with a whistling bird singing inside. This tiara is a tad more subtle, but it makes a strong statement for the queen who's not afraid of drawing a bit of attention.

The idea was hatched with the discovery of a sweet plastic bird found at a Sunday morning flea market. After that, creating was a "piece of cake," as Queen Marie might have said.

This tiara would be fun for anyone, but it's especially designed for that friend with an impressive vocal talent. A songbird...the princess of pitch-perfect pipes.

Make Your Own
{queen of extreme}

Directives

1. Create tiara base made with ½" paper strips cut from page from a fairy tale book and a thin headband (see tiara instructions, page 114).

2. Cut three pieces of decorative cardstock: two strips about 4" x ½" that taper to width of headband for sides of tiara and one piece about 4" x 3" with three rounded peaks for the front.

3. Decoupage book page and sheet music to cardstock pieces using foam brush and craft glue; let dry.

4. Trim edges of cardstock pieces and then adhere to headband using double-sided tape.

5. Adhere jewel to paper flower using craft glue. Using photo as your guide, adhere velvet leaves, jeweled embellishment threaded with ribbon, and vintage bird to front of tiara using dimensional adhesive.

6. Edge leaves and tiara peaks with glitter gel.

Tools & Adhesives
- craft glue
- double-sided tape
- foam brush
- glitter gel
- paper scissors
- ruler
- water-based dimensional adhesive

Royal Trimmings
- decorative cardstock
- fairy tale book page
- jewel
- jeweled embellishment
- old sheet music
- paper flower
- plastic bird
- ribbon
- thin plastic headband
- velvet leaves

Her Royal
Highness
of
Happiness

*S*he's the one who always knows exactly what to say when you feel like the world is out to get you. When it rains, she is convinced that sunny skies are just a few insignificant clouds away. She believes that people are essentially good, that the express line will really be faster than all the other lines, and that anything is possible with a little pixie dust and elbow grease. In short, she is mightily worthy of the Fairy Princess tiara.

What is a fairy princess? This lovely being possesses magical powers and embodies the spirit of goodwill to all who are fortunate enough to believe.

She would wear a tiara such as this one, created with antique embossed wallpaper for the base, a vintage Bakelite shoe clip for the centerpiece, and lots of added sparkle. The trim of this delicate headpiece is reminiscent of Lily-of-the-Valley, blooms reflecting the eternal optimist's belief that spring is always just around the corner. The finishing touch is a vintage watch casing with a tiny fairy inlay, placed front and center on the peak of this whimsical wonder.

The wearer of this tiara transcends from the mortal world and gains her rightful place next to all the other good fairies.

Make Your Own
{her royal highness of happiness}

Directives

1. Glue 2" strip of cardstock to plastic headband from end to end with hot glue.

2. Cut embossed wallpaper into three triangular pieces about 5" wide at base and 6" high.

3. Use hot glue to adhere one triangular piece to the front center of headband and the other two pieces to the front sides of headband. The pieces will overlap.

4. Adhere upholstery cord piping to bottom of headband with hot glue.

5. Cut triangular piece of wallpaper 7" wide at base and 8" tall. Adhere to inside center of crown with hot glue.

6. Paint inside of crown with gold floral spray to give it a finished look.

7. Add gimp trim along bottom edge of headband base with hot glue.

8. Glue fairy picture inside watch face. Embellish watch face rim with rhinestones. Glue to decorative metal stamping.

9. Affix watch face and jewelry on top point of tallest triangular piece. For extra support, wrap with wire and poke wire ends through back of paper; twist wire to secure.

10. Spray tongue depressor with gold floral spray; let dry. Adhere with hot glue to center of back triangular wallpaper piece for support. Glue tongue depressor over wire twist used to secure watch face embellishment.

11. Hot glue various embellishments in a pleasing design on crown front. Use rhinestones to highlight floral motifs as desired.

Tools & Adhesives

- fabric scissors
- hot-glue gun
- paper scissors

Royal Trimmings

- cardstock, 15" x 2"
- charms
- earrings
- embossed wallpaper
- fairy picture
- filigree
- gimp trim, beige
- gold floral spray
- metal stamping
- plastic headband
- rhinestones
- shoe clip
- thin craft wire
- tongue depressor
- upholstery cord piping, beige, ½" x 15"
- watch face

Principesa *of* Parties

*E*ven when she isn't wearing a lamp-shade on her head, the ultimate party girl is easy to spot. Here's what to look for:

- Her phone is never picked up before 11 on a Sunday morning.
- Friends must book their reservation weeks in advance for a Friday night get-together, months ahead if it's the holiday season.
- Even the most mundane of party games comes alive when she decides to join in.

The party girl can play piano, sing, do the tango, and play Twister better than the average 5-year-old. She can make box wine taste like champagne and turn the deadliest bore into a wit for the night. A party just isn't any fun without her.

This crown is a party hat that tells every-one when it's time to dance, and when it's time to go home (that would be when the crown is on the dog).

Make Your Own
{principesa of parties}

Directives

1. Form 12" x 16" piece of French sheet music into cone shape; secure with double-stick tape. Embellish images on paper with glitter gels.

2. Adhere cone to inside of 2" x 14" metal band wrapped with tinsel trim using foam dots.

3. Roll tinsel garland into a ball to fit securely on top of cone; secure in place with craft glue.

4. Adhere velvet leaves on top of garland using craft glue.

Tools & Adhesives
- craft glue
- double-stick tape
- foam dots
- ruler

Royal Trimmings
- French sheet music
- glitter gels
- metal band
- tinsel garland
- velvet leaves

*"On with the dance! let joy be unconfined.
No sleep till morn, when Youth and Pleasure meet
To chase the glowing hours with flying feet."*

– Childe Harold's Pilgimage by George Gordon Byron

Countess of Creative Chaos

There *is* such a thing as happy chaos. In fact, as many artists know, a messy desk, room, barn, or studio is often the place to achieve the most.

While artists know this and have long since come to terms with their clutter, care must be taken in proclaiming someone the Countess of Creative Chaos. Tidiness is a virtue (so they say) and most women try their whole lives to attain it. They may not take this high compliment in quite the same spirit it was intended.

The crown, however, will smooth their ruffled feathers. Who could resist its feminine simplicity? Starting with wrapping paper, a crown-shaped piece is adhered to 1-ply museum board. Three points are embellished with accordion-pleated rosettes and foil embellishments, and a glittering title—oh, like Queen, for instance—is in the crown's center.

The lesson here is that while the surroundings may appear messy, the crown itself is testament to an active and creative mind that is always making silk purses and lemonade.

Make Your Own
{countess of creative chaos}

Directives

1. Trace desired crown pattern on wrapping paper. Pay attention to placement of pattern to ensure details on wrapping paper are positioned where you want them. Cut out crown pattern, leaving about ¼" around circumference of pattern.

2. Apply double-sided tape around edges of underside of wrapping paper. Adhere wrapping paper to museum board. Cut out crown with scissors.

3. Using computer, print crown title in black. Line up crown pattern over printed title and trace title with pencil. (Use a light box or large flashlight if the printed title is hard to see under the wrapping paper.)

4. Using fine-tip adhesive applicator, outline and completely fill in crown title with glitter adhesive. Generously sprinkle glitter over adhesive.

5. To assemble rosettes: Cut out wrapping paper with pinking shears using the following measurements: 7" x ½" (cut 2); 7" x 2" (cut 2); 7" x 2 ½" (cut 1). Fold paper into ¼" folds accordion-style. Staple center of rosette or tie with wire. Spread open ends of rosette and hot glue ends together to make a circle.

6. Apply rosettes to points on crown using hot glue. Place largest rosette on the middle point, smallest rosettes on outside points, and medium rosettes on outer middle points. Hot glue Dresdens to center of each rosette.

7. Punch holes in both sides of crown. Cut two 8" lengths of ribbon; attach to holes on either side of crown and use to fasten ends of crown together.

Tools & Adhesives
- computer and printer
- double-sided tape
- glitter adhesive with fine-tip applicator
- hole punch
- hot-glue gun
- paper scissors
- pencil
- pinking shears
- ruler
- stapler

Royal Trimmings
- 1-ply museum board
- Dresden pieces
- German glass glitter
- ribbon
- wrapping paper

Monarch of Memories

Someone once said that "a man's home is his castle" and yet the woman is often the mortar that holds it all together. She's usually the one who also makes sure her children understand their roots in the family tree. Think of all the scrapbooks made over the years and give a silent "thank you" to the hands that took time to preserve family heritage.

The Family Circle crown may appear fanciful and frivolous, but it is actually a profound tribute to ancestors and the familial ties that bind. Family members of both husband and wife are represented on this crown, with cutout wedding and other special occasion photos.

An old piece of lamp trim forms the base, which is then built upon with wired pieces of jewelry. Connecting each photo are vintage watch faces that suggest the fleetness of time.

The Family Circle crown will always be unique, an apt reflection of the memories in each family that are irreplaceable.

Make Your Own
{monarch of memories}

Directives

1. Color copy family photos onto cream cardstock; cut out and glue onto matt board (sturdy enough to support photos, flexible enough to cut). Make five groups of photos. Cut out using craft knife.

2. Punch holes and attach eyelets to photos—one eyelet at the top, one at the knee section of each photo side. Wire photos to jewelry piece on top and watch face on the bottom at connection, thus wiring all the photos together in a circle. Add bullion and ribbon. Wire all photos together in a circle repeating the procedure above.

3. The lamp trim should have a folded edge, so just open it up a bit and tuck the photos into the fold; pinch it tightly to hold them in place.

4. Add crepe paper fan shape to bottom of each photo grouping with hot glue. Sprinkle embossing powder along bottom curve of fan and emboss with heat tool. Hot glue crown-shaped jewelry pieces to top of some of the fans.

5. Make crepe paper circles; embellish with embossing powder and glitter in the center.

6. Glue tongue depressor behind each photo group, placing photos at bottom of depressor. For variety, glue piece of sheet music to half of depressor (vertically). Glue one crepe paper circle to top of each depressor.

7. Cut stars out of cardstock and embellish with glitter. Attach star to back of crepe paper circle with hot glue.

Tools & Adhesives
- craft knife
- craft wire
- eyelet setting tools
- glitter adhesive
- heat tool
- hole punch
- hot-glue gun
- paper scissors
- photocopier
- white craft glue

Royal Trimmings
- bullion
- cream cardstock
- Dresden circles
- embossing powder
- eyelets
- family photos
- German glass glitter
- matt board
- old jewelry bits, lamp trim
- ribbon
- tongue depressors, 5
- vintage crepe paper
- vintage sheet music
- watch faces, 5

Queen Mother

*C*onsider the sparrow, who spends much of her short life building nests for her young, waiting for the young to arrive, then endlessly flying on food-gathering missions. Talk about keeping it all together.

While this gorgeous crown, literally bursting with soaring birds, glittering branches, and pearly clusters of eggs, is a fitting tribute to a first-time mom, consider bestowing it on a more seasoned mother as well.

The Queen Mother may not have a clean shirt to her name and considers "fancy restaurant" an oxymoron, but with her splendid circlet of flora and fauna, she will always be reminded that she wouldn't trade her life for a kingdom.

Make Your Own
{queen mother}

Directives

1. Create the base of this crown with posterboard cut into stylized points. Add layer of glitter adhesive and then sprinkle with ice blue glass glitter.

2. Adhere angel hair tinsel around the perimeter to resemble a nest, then attach branches with hot glue.

3. Sprinkle bird wings with silver glass glitter. Cut wire into various lengths and hot glue birds to the tops. Adhere wired birds to the crown base, and then strategically scatter eggs and glue in place.

Tools & Adhesives
- craft scissors
- glitter adhesive
- hot-glue gun
- wire cutters

Royal Trimmings
- angel hair tinsel
- cotton batting birds
- fine-gauge wire
- ice blue, silver German glass glitter
- posterboard
- small painted eggs
- various size millinery branches

"In raising my children, I have lost my mind but found my soul."

—Lisa T. Shepherd

Merry Queen
of Snapshots

New kingdoms have formed in cities, suburbs, and rural areas everywhere, and yet the rulers toil uncrowned. They are artists and archivists, women who not only cherish the memories but also spend many hours building great illustrated books of photographs and mementos.

Most know them as scrapbookers, but anyone who has been sucked into the gentle vortex of pasting photos and searching for just the right embellishment knows that it is truly a way of life.

An avid scrapbooker would proudly wear her Remember Me tiara, which recalls memories of her own youth as well as urges both ruler and subjects to capture each moment they can. With its headband base festooned in soft loops of ribbon, the tiara ascends with multiple layers of pleated rosettes. At the center, a Victorian child with her own crown holds a doll and beseeches all to "remember me."

Childhood vanishes quickly; anyone who strives to preserve its essence deserves a tiara and a throne.

Make Your Own
{merry queen of snapshots}

Directives

1. Wrap headband in plain ribbon and secure with hot glue at each end.

2. Cut out cardstock in a mountain shape 5" tall in the center and tapering to about 1" on each side. Cover with printed paper using spray glue. Cut a decorative edge on the top curved edge. Center and glue to outside of headband.

3. Accordion fold 7" x 10" piece of printed paper. Fold in half and secure in the center with fine wire. Cut ends on the diagonal. Fan out folds and secure center with clear tape. Glue to center of crown about 1½" up from the bottom.

4. Cut cream crepe paper into two pieces about 6" x 10"; gather and secure center with fine wire. Fluff out and cut edges with decorative-edge scissors; nestle on either side behind the accordion fold and then glue in place.

5. Cut 5" x 10" piece of tan crepe paper. Gather and secure in center with fine wire. Fluff out and cut edges with decorative-edge scissors; glue centered on top of accordion fold.

6. Cut out vintage photo either around the image or in an oval shape. Glue printed paper wings and a pointy cap to image. Trim wings and cap with glue and sprinkle on glass glitter. Glue to front of crown.

7. Tie brown ribbon in a bow; glue to center of crown under image. Arrange bow and tails into artful swirls and swoops towards back; glue to secure. Either handwrite or computer generate "Remember Me" on paper banner. Cut decorative edges. Gently bend banner and glue on either side of image.

Tools & Adhesives

- clear tape
- decorative-edge scissors
- glue dots
- hot-glue gun
- spray glue

Royal Trimmings

- 1½" yards brown ribbbon
- 15" x 5" heavy cardstock
- copy of vintage photo
- cream, tan crepe paper
- fabric-covered headband
- fine wire
- German glass glitter
- paper banner
- plain ribbon
- vintage printed paper

Estate secrets

Fancy Flourishes
Hints for an amazing scrapbooker's tiara.

- Glue decorative paper to cardstock on both sides before cutting the front piece.
- Cut the ends of accordion-pleated rosettes at a slant for a star-like effect.
- Use a heavier ribbon for the loops and bows; it will hold its shape better.
- To glitter the Victorian child's wings, use a glue pen to make fine outlines.

Countess One-of-a-Kind

*P*art of the appeal of old jewelry is its elaborate detail. The master craftsmen who made it knew a thing or two about guilloche and repousse and many other impressive techniques with splendid French names. Such amazing artistry is something to be savored and heralded, just like that special someone who abhors conformity and who never ceases to amaze with her wit and style.

This dazzling filigree crown brings to mind the craftsmanship of old and should encircle the head of a true original. The maker of this royal diadem pays tribute to its extraordinary wearer by using a special kind of craft ribbon with an amazing filigree pattern built right in.

This vision of sparkle is the simplest crown to create, but here is a little secret: It is a lot of look with little effort, time, or money. You can get very creative with this project by cutting more designs out of the ribbon and building up the front. Use your imagination, for the sky is truly your only limit.

Make Your Own
{countess one-of-a-kind}

Directives

1. Measure enough gold filigree craft ribbon to fit around the head. Cut off top to make the border.

2. Attach semi-firm wire to bottom of border using hot glue. Cover wire with thin gold ribbon.

3. For added sparkle, spray crown with mounting adhesive and sprinkle with opalescent glitter.

Tools & Adhesives

- craft scissors
- hot-glue gun
- spray mount adhesive
- wire cutters

Royal Trimmings

- 16-gauge wire
- gold filigree craft ribbon
- opalescent glitter
- thin gold ribbon

Duchess *of* Delightful Differences

Most clubs exist to acknowledge similarities among its members. But in the club of mother and daughter, friend and friend, or sister and sister, it's often the differences that are the only thing in common. It may cause some disagreements and squabbling but it sure makes life more interesting.

Inspired by a chance comment on how different a mother felt her daughter was and yet how much she loved to spend time with her, this Birds of Different Feathers crown is a happy testament to the many faces of friendship and love. The main characters are charming birds taken from old prints, photocopied and given little wire feet. They look quite at home on a lush background of apple branches and blossoms.

A good queen knows how to get along with all of her subjects, no matter how odd they might be. Perhaps this crown could be given to that special someone who, though she walks to the beat of a different drum, knows how to cherish the individuality of the loved ones in her life.

Make Your Own
{duchess of delightful differences}

Directives

1. To create crown base: Shape frame using thick florist wire. Wrap with green crepe paper cut into ½" strips and adhere ends with craft glue.

2. Create blossoms, buds, and leaves (see Crepe Paper Magic, page 85); attach to crown base.

3. Photocopy bird prints, right side and mirror image. Cut out birds and glue back to back with end of 4" piece of 22-gauge wire sandwiched in between. Wire birds onto crown where desired.

Tools & Adhesives

- computer and printer
- craft glue
- floral tape
- paper scissors

Royal Trimmings

- 22-gauge wire
- bird prints
- moss green, pink, yellow crepe paper
- thick florist's wire

"Originality exists in every individual because each of us differs from the others. We are all primary numbers divisible only by ourselves."

—Jean Guitton

Crepe Paper Magic

Use techniques from yesteryear to create beautiful apple blossoms.

The buds and blossoms on this crown were made using instructions from a vintage pattern. For each blossom, a strip of five petals is cut from white or pale pink crepe paper, a leaf pattern from moss green crepe paper, a calyx from light green crepe paper, and a yellow center made from a strip of yellow crepe paper clipped into a fine fringe. For the buds, simply cover a small ball of pink crepe paper with a square of the same color, stretching it smoothly. Wrap base with 4" length of thin wire. Brush with glue and attach a green calyx around it. To finish, wrap all stems with ½"-wide strips of moss green crepe paper.

Baroness of Bon Voyage

There is nothing more entertaining than peeking into the lives of those around us—in a purely innocent form, of course. It's delightful to catch a glimpse of the lives of others through a front window or to witness a happy group dining al fresco on the front porch. You can't get those vignettes from a speeding car—no, take a cue from the famous flaneuses of France and explore the heart of every town and city that you can on foot.

To celebrate the woman who owns two pairs of walking shoes and knows how to use them, a strolling crown pays tribute to her wanderlust. Covered in vintage French text, this crown is adorned with velvet ribbon, velvet flowers, hand-dyed silk ribbon, and pompoms that mark each step with a lively jiggle. In the center, an illustration of inspiration is placed— images of beautiful bridges in Paris that must be walked over to be truly savored.

Yes, a sun hat would be much more practical for the Strolling Queen but nowhere near as fun. And as the endlessly fascinating scenery rolls by, the Queen should remember with joy that she has just added to it.

Make Your Own
{baroness of bon voyage}

Directives

1. Adhere four to six book pages (preferably French) to 24" x 8" piece of posterboard using mounting adhesive. Cut out illustration with decorative-edge scissors and attach to center using glue stick.

2. Cut out crown shape, making numerous pointed peaks.

3. Cut six 8" lengths of 22-gauge wire. Using needle-nose pliers or your fingers, create spirals and attach to peaks of crown by taping them to the back. Wrap velvet flowers around wires and tie with ribbon.

4. Apply velvet ribbon and pompom fringe to base of crown with craft glue. Bring edges of crown together and secure with double-sided tape.

5. Add velvet flowers to edges of illustration and glue in place.

Tools & Adhesives
- craft glue
- decorative-edge scissors
- double-sided tape
- glue stick
- mounting adhesive
- needle-nose pliers
- paper scissors
- wire cutters

Royal Trimmings
- 22-gauge wire
- pompom fringe
- posterboard
- ribbon
- velvet flowers
- velvet ribbon
- vintage book pages
- vintage illustration

Estate Secrets

Picture Perfect

Places to find the perfect vintage illustration.

Plenty of beautiful scenery from the past exists to create your crown centerpiece. You just need to know where to look. Start with trusty eBay, where thousands of pieces of ephemera are for sale every day.

There are also many vintage paper shows—check the Internet or antiques periodicals for show dates and times.

Flea markets and antique shops also carry lots of old illustrated periodicals and print books. Don't overlook old postcards and advertisements.

Finally, consider reproduction books with lots of images that often include a CD for easy downloading.

Belle of the Ball Jugglers

If a busy schedule sounds familiar and you're not yet wearing a crown to signify your mastery of multitasking, then you better add "make a tiara" to your list of things to do.

This tiara is a tribute to all of us who make magic happen every day—the magic of keeping it all together in the face of tremendous odds.

The one good thing about getting older is that it takes a pretty smart cookie to keep up with it all. If you ever doubt the value you bring to the table, think back to the last time you went away for a few days and left someone else in charge. It wasn't pretty, was it?

Make Your Own
{belle of the ball jugglers}

Directives

1. Photocopy all images for tiara, including mother, three children, owl, top hat, scrolls, and florals.

2. Decoupage book text onto one side of cardstock and scroll images onto opposite side; let dry. Cut out 2" x 12" strip with decorative-edge scissors. This will be the band of the tiara.

3. Decoupage mother figure onto cardstock. On opposite side decoupage floral wallpaper; let dry then cut out. Follow same procedure for decorative florals, hat, owl, and children onto third piece of cardstock.

4. Adhere mother figure to tiara base with craft glue; clamp to hold in place and let dry. Attach all remaining pieces where desired with craft glue.

5. To attach children, poke hole through mother's dress and one through child's head with needle. Loop 2" piece of 22-gauge wire through child's head; attach to dress and pinch loop closed with needle-nose pliers; trim wire if necessary.

6. Cut out bottom center of dress to create a cove, about 1½" x 2". Using scrap of book text and scroll cardstock (from tiara band section), cut 2½" x 2" piece; fold ¼" up around three sides, leaving bottom edge flat, and cut across this edge with decorative-edge scissors. Attach behind cove with craft glue and clamp until dry.

7. Attach small child under skirt using wire. Embellish tiara wih beads, millinery flowers, and jewelry as desired.

Tools & Adhesives

- craft glue
- craft scissors
- decorative-edge scissors
- decoupage medium
- foam brush
- needle-nose pliers
- photocopier
- small clamps
- wire cutters

Royal Trimmings

- 22-gauge wire
- beads
- book text
- cardstock, 3
- jewelry remnants
- millinery flowers
- scroll images
- vintage bird, people images, lace, trims, feathers, floral wallpaper

Aside from their very practical purpose of opening locks, keys are a telling symbol of both keeping secrets and knowing the answers.

The worthy wearer of this key-encrusted crown, then, is the friend who can be trusted with your deepest secrets. She locks away your whispered confidences for safekeeping, never to tell a soul. The trustworthy Sorceress of Secrets is a rare gem because she understands the importance of secure alliances and refuses to feed the royal grapevine. With her, a secret is always safe.

Make Your Own
{sorceress of secrets}

Directives

1. The "key" to this crown is finding old skeleton keys of various lengths and designs. Even old wind-up keys would work splendidly. The base is posterboard cut with an artist's cutting blade, then painted and stained (with acrylic paint, polyurethane, floral, and wood stains) to look like oxidized metal.

2. Keys are laid out in a pleasing pattern and woven together with fine gunmetal wire then attached to the base with craft wire. Mysterious touches include mercury glass sequins and bits of velvet from an antique ceremonial robe. Adhere these with epoxy and hot glue.

Tools & Adhesives
- artist's cutting blade
- epoxy
- hot-glue gun
- wire cutters

Royal Trimmings
- craft wire
- fine gunmetal wire
- floral spray stain
- mercury glass sequins
- polyurethane spray
- posterboard
- silver spray paint
- skeleton and windup vintage keys
- velvet scraps
- wood spray stain

Sovereign Tea

The tradition of teatime is a long and storied one. Portuguese Catherine of Braganza (1638–1705), queen consort to King Charles II of England, is credited with making tea a favorite pastime in England by the late 1600s. Children especially loved to engage in the ritualistic pouring of tea and passing delicate edibles to their friends and dolls gathered together in the nursery.

A Royal Tea tiara, then, is a wonderful mix of childhood relics and grown-up vintage chic. Every element on this unique tiara should be old, or tea-stained, or both. Think of the look of a hat that has been fished out from an old trunk in the attic; it is worn when friends gather for tea and conversation.

Heavy wire is formed into a base with a single arch in the front; look for some vintage beads that might be a bit tarnished but in a wonderful shape and muted color. These are threaded onto wire, with antique tinsel and crinkle-wire wound throughout. A china doll's head smiles down on the proceedings; she wishes "Bonne Fete" to all of the guests who raise their cups to the Queen of Teatime. Rising over all, a glittering star brings good wishes to every guest at the end of a delightful afternoon.

Make Your Own
{sovereign tea}

Directives

1. Cut 12" length of 20-gauge wire and thread it with ten glass beads. Gently bend to a rainbow curve.

2. String remaining beads evenly on 16-gauge wire, leaving about 6" for doll head. Gently bend into a circle the size of your head; twist and secure ends of wire. Attach curved 20-gauge wire to base.

3. Twist vintage tinsel around free 6" portion of wire. Secure ends with a bit of craft glue.

4. Wrap crinkle wire to form a fan beginning in center of crown and radiating out towards the edges of curve.

5. Cut a pair of wings from printed paper. Glue to back of doll head. Glue Dresden trim around her head. Gently place doll head in center of crown and glue in place with craft glue. Write "Bonne Fete" or your own special saying on paper banner and glue to front of doll.

6. Cut a star from black cardstock. Glue 16-gauge wire stem to star. Cover star with glitter adhesive on both sides and apply glass glitter; when dry, affix to top center of crown with hot glue.

7. Make two rosettes of crepe paper and glue to either side of crown. Double the ribbon and tie in a bow at the back to cover the twisted wire.

Tools & Adhesives
- black permanent marker
- craft glue
- glitter adhesive
- hot-glue gun
- wire cutters

Royal Trimmings
- 1" vintage glass beads (about 28)
- 2" vintage china doll head with shoulder plate
- 3" paper for banner
- 16-gauge black wire
- 20-gauge wire
- black cardstock
- bronze German glass glitter
- cream crepe paper
- crinkle wire
- Dresden trim
- printed paper scrap
- ribbon, 1½ yard

"*I am a princess. All girls are. Even if they live in tiny, old attics, even if they dress in rags, even if they aren't pretty, or smart, or young. They're still princesses. All of us.*"

– "*A Little Princess*"
by Frances Hodgson Burnett

Princess of Prose

For centuries, women who dared to write were often compelled to use pen names—even Jane Austen originally published her works "By a Lady." It was thought unseemly for the weaker sex to be so much in the public eye—rather vulgar, you know, especially for the upper classes.

Times have changed, thank heavens. Today, if a woman is fortunate enough to have a talent for prose, she's going to shout it from the rooftops. No hiding behind pen names or feelings of shame; only visions of book signings and literary fame dance as the fingers type, type, type. Therefore, why not advertise this enviable penchant for the pen with a quill-studded tiara?

For the writer in your life (or inside yourself), try this on for size: a silver tiara with a giant glittering feather that symbolizes the power writing has given to women over the centuries. An ornate brass charm (a buckle would work well, too) is painted silver and attached to a simple silver tiara base. Rising high into the air, a glittering silver plume tells husband, children, and other distractions that there is a writer hard at work on her next masterpiece.

Make Your Own
{princess of prose}

Directives

1. Cut 1"-wide strip of silver handmade paper. Hot glue end of strip to inside end of headband at 30-degree angle with ¾" tab overhang. Fold and tuck tab and sides of tab over end of headband and tack with hot glue. Staying at 30-degree angle, coat underside of strip with white glue and wrap tightly around headband until you reach the end. If one strip of paper is not long enough connect another to end of first strip and continue wrapping entire headband. Cut off excess paper, leaving a ¾" tab overhang. Tuck and fold tab over end of headband and tack with hot glue.

2. To color brass ornament, lightly coat with silver buffing polish using a stiff paintbrush and polish with a soft cloth. Add second layer of polish and repeat previous steps. Coat edges of ornament with thin line of craft glue and dust with glass glitter. Hot glue brass ornament to center of headband.

3. If artificial feather is bright color, spray paint silver to provide a nice background for glitter. When dry, coat one side with craft glue that has been slightly thinned with water. Coat with glass glitter. When dry, coat other side of feather. Hot glue feather to inside of brass ornament.

Tools & Adhesives
- hot-glue gun
- paintbrush
- paper scissors
- white craft glue

Royal Trimmings
- artificial feather
- brass ornament
- fine silver glass glitter
- silver buffing polish
- silver handmade cloth-like paper or silver ribbon
- silver spray paint
- thin plastic headband

"There's a story to nearly everything, it just takes the right person to convey it in words. I would venture to guess that Anon, who wrote so many poems without signing them, was often a woman."

—Virginia Woolf

*I*s there such a thing as too much glitter? Depends on who is being asked. If it's a woman between the ages of 2 and 102 who believes in fairy dust and has watched *Ziegfeld Follies* at least twice, the answer is pretty obvious.

A healthy dose of glitter is all it takes to attain the ultimate level of sublime and, dare we say, a tiny touch of "Drama Queen" in this outrageously gorgeous crown.

For the woman who likes to "dress up," has the coolest array of evening bags, and has never been the same since elbow-length gloves went out of fashion, the Glitterati crown will feel right at home on her stylish head.

With a hint of Mardi Gras and a whole bunch of attitude, the Glitterati crown is sure to draw stares of profound appreciation. After all, it's no fun to be Queen if you can't dress like you own a treasury or two, right?

Make Your Own
{grand duchess of sparkle & shine}

Directives

1. Beginning with a 20" x 8" piece of posterboard, cut into desired shape for the base; sprinkle liberally with silver and gold glitter. Glue short ends together with hot glue.

2. Add glitter to the millinery swords, then twist them into spirals and glue them to the base. Add rhinestone sprays, pearl bouquet picks, and miniature birds mounted on wire.

3. Adhere several strands of vintage wax pearls around bottom of the base.

4. Print a title (like Queen of the Lovelies) on a piece of cardstock, cut decoratively and adhere to the center of crown.

Tools & Adhesives

- craft scissors
- glitter adhesive
- hot-glue gun

Royal Trimmings

- cardstock
- millinery sword ferns
- pearl bouquet picks
- posterboard
- silver, gold German glass glitter
- small cotton birds
- vintage rhinestone sprays, wax pearls
- wire

Crown & Glory

Most women have a weakness for jewelry—but for some it is a slight madness. Families have been torn apart from tussling over a bit of superheated carbon. Massive arguments over Great-Grandma's baroque pearl brooch have divided sisters for decades. Entire paychecks have been secretly spent on a fabulous amethyst pendant or an unforgettable hair comb made of gold, sapphires, and seed pearls.

If there is a 12-step program for jewel junkies, then this hypnotized heiress is a prime candidate. But first, she must don the official tiara—as Bling Queen, Protector of the Jewel-Rich and Cash-Poor everywhere.

Luckily the tiara itself won't land its creator in debtor's prison. Once again, it's made from castoff costume jewelry and clearance sale finds that come together in a dashing explosion of faceted splendor. The base is a simple plastic tiara ready to be filled with various pieces of earrings, necklaces, and brooches.

Whether one only dreams of being draped in diamonds and gold or actually has a reserved parking spot at Tiffany's, there is a tiara with royalty written all over it waiting to be donned. Once it's placed on the rightful recipient's head, she is sure to have good health, good luck, and good fortune for the rest of her days.

Make Your Own
{crown & glory}

Directives

1. Remove the shanks and backs from all jewelry and arrange everything in the design you want. The jewelry should cover the entire front and sides of the tiara.

2. Using epoxy, adhere each piece onto the tiara. Fill in with rhinestones.

Tools & Adhesives
- epoxy
- rhinestone grabber
- shank nippers

Royal Trimmings
- plastic tiara
- rhinestones
- various earrings, buttons, brooches

Birthday Baroness

Back in the days of youth when becoming a year older was an event to be celebrated rather than suppressed, a little girl was indeed the queen of the day in her best dress and patent leather shoes.

Rewind the mind for a few moments to the days before pizza parlors and inflatable play structures were the highlight of a natal day. A childhood birthday party was anticipated for weeks and could have been nothing more than memory games, musical chairs, and a chance to pin the tail on the donkey.

After these heady activities, a slice of honest-to-goodness homemade cake, ice cream, and a gaily-colored paper cup of nuts and candies to bring home made the whole divine occasion complete.

This tribute to birthdays past has a cartoon-like crown shape in the front, built on a simple base. A strip of festive decorative cardstock (polka dot in this case) is cut into classical crown points and a festive cupcake is front and center, with frosting made of chiffon ribbon. The clown is a vintage cupcake pick.

This classic Natal Day tiara is a nostalgic tribute to all the birthday princesses of the past who, though they might today succumb to the modern-day pressures of high-tech entertainment for their own children, secretly yearn for the simple celebrations of yesteryear when her age was no secret.

Make Your Own
{birthday baroness}

Directives

1. Starting with a tiara base made with ½" paper strips cut from pages of an old book and a thin headband (see tiara instructions, page 114), cut and adhere 12" x 6" piece of decorative cardstock cut with five peaks at the top to create base.

2. Cut cupcake shape from yellow paper; glue to tiara with dimensional adhesive. Embellish with birthday text. Outline text with glitter gel.

3. Form top of cupcake shape using pink chiffon ribbon, adhering with dimensional adhesive.

4. Adhere pink Dresden wheel, plastic clown pick, and silver stars to front of base using dimensional adhesive.

5. Add bursts of pink tinsel to the tops of each crown point and around base using craft glue. Add silver Dresden trim on top of tinsel at base.

Tools & Adhesives
- craft glue
- paper scissors
- ruler
- water-based dimensional adhesive

Royal Trimmings
- birthday definition text
- decorative cardstock, polka dot and yellow
- glitter gel
- old book pages
- paper strips
- pink chiffon ribbon
- pink Dresden wheel
- pink tinsel garland
- plastic clown on pick
- silver Dresden trim
- silver stars
- thin plastic headband

Estate Secrets

Pass It On
Share your birthday tiara with
a few good friends.

A joyous tiara like this must be passed around.
Together with a close group of friends who
celebrate birthdays together, let each birthday
girl wear the tiara on her special day, then give
it to the next celebrant. With each passing, the
tiara should have an additional embellishment
added so that it becomes grander and grander.
It just goes to show that one does not get older,
just better accessorized.

Starry Tsarina

Perhaps you or one of your closest friends has an extraordinary fascination with astral planes and descending planets. When this old world needs fixing and most ordinary citizens hide behind their TVs to watch the news, the Starry Tsarina looks heavenward, consults her charts, and draws the ever-comforting conclusion that it is all indeed written in the stars.

This prismatic crown casts a glow like the Northern Lights in an evening sky. The allure of this crown is entrancing; eyes are captivated by the beautiful colors that bounce off the bands of iridescence. In fact, they just make you want more. It's the perfect headdress for the woman who keeps a close and protective watch on the universe.

It all begins with an embossed wallpaper trim. The trim is hand-painted a soft baby blue and then lightly dusted with iridescent glitter. The base is layered with bands of trim with silver tones and lots of sparkle.

The crown face is decorated with a sensational star-shaped ornament as well as vintage rhinestone jewelry and buttons and dangling crystals. The cascading beaded garland is a fitting nod to the twinkling lights dancing in the evening sky. From top to bottom, this crown is spectacularly stunning...some might say, out of this world.

Make Your Own
{starry tsarina}

Directives

1. Using a 15" wallpaper border, cut out design along the top; hot glue end to end and spray lightly with pale blue floral spray paint.

2. Spray the whole crown with hairspray and sprinkle iridescent glitter, working quickly as it dries fast.

3. Starting from the back and working your way around, add trims and ribbons with hot glue. Glue iridescent crystal ornament to paper in center with hot glue.

4. Cut a 10" piece of 20-gauge wire and bend in half, forming a hairpin. Poke it from back to front and wire the brooch through its cutwork openings. Leaving the wire long, add beads and crystals; fold ends.

5. Cut two pieces of beaded garland and hot glue on the back side of the crown. Use hot glue to attach brooch, wire, and two beaded strands. Bend strands down slightly to form wings. Tack to sides with hot glue. Tack two more pieces of beaded wire to top sides with hot glue, letting ends dangle free.

6. Embellish with rhinestones. (Clear glitter from each spot before gluing.) Mount rhinestones on clear buttons and glue along bottom front.

Tools & Adhesives

- craft glue
- craft scissors
- hairspray
- hot-glue gun
- rhinestone grabber
- wire cutters

Royal Trimmings

- 20-gauge wire
- beaded garland spray
- beads
- crystals
- iridescent crystal ornament
- iridescent glitter
- pale blue floral spray paint
- rhinestones
- star and moon brooch
- various trims, ribbons
- wallpaper border
- white crystal buttons

Estate Secrets

Double Dipping

Get the biggest glam from
your glitter with this trick.

When using glitter, you'll encounter a trade-off.
Finer glitter is much easier to work with, but it
doesn't sparkle as brilliantly as coarser glitter.

Here's what to do: Thin craft glue with water
and apply; layer with fine glitter. Then apply a
second coat of glue and add a second layer of
coarse glitter. Each individual flake reflects more
light and will provide lots of sparkle, while the
double layers ensure even coverage.

WICKED

On sunny days, when all is right with the world, the dark side of the moon casts no shadow. But everyone has her moments and for that Queen of the Macabre in your life, the Corpse Bride is like a sister.

The Queen of the Macabre loves the strange, the spooky, and the creepy. Her world is not always a sunny place with bluebirds chirping at her window and skies filled with cotton candy clouds.

This charmed tiara seems to be spun from a black widow's web, perfect for the "wicked" princess who lives inside. It's nothing short of the perfect finishing touch on a Halloween costume.

It's never been more fashionable to flaunt your spooky side. Delicate spiderwebs, creepy dolls' heads, and lots of sparkling crystals are easily mixed into a crown or tiara that is truly to die for.

Make Your Own
{queen of screams}

Directives

1. Cut two pieces of 16-gauge wire approximately 21" long. Using needle-nose pliers, twist them together to form a circle to fit your head. Bend ends into loops and flatten blunt points as much as possible. If desired, thread ribbon through each loop so the wearer can adjust the fit.

2. With 30" piece of 19-gauge wire, form series of loops until you come up with something you like. (This is the point where you can scratch yourself easily so be careful.) You may need to use more than one piece to get all the way around the head form. Don't be afraid to play around with the wire until you get the hang of it.

3. Cut small pieces of 22-gauge wire to wrap design to the headpiece. This will take several pieces, and you may need to wire parts of the designs together for extra support.

4. Embellish with doll head, letter tiles, crystals, or whatever spooky whimsy you wish. Wire or hot glue everything in place.

Tools & Adhesives
- hot-glue gun
- needle-nose pliers
- ruler
- safety glasses
- wire cutters

Royal Trimmings
- 16-, 19-, 22-gauge wire
- doll head
- letter tiles
- ribbon
- various-size crystals

Making a Base

Many of the crowns and tiaras in this book were made with either a paper base or a metal (wire) base. Paper-based tiaras are often built on a standard plastic headband and covered in ribbon or paper. The following are the two basic methods of building the base that will become your crown.

Paper Base Crown or Tiara

You can make a crown completely of paper or start with a different base and work off that. Begin with a sturdy base. This could be a fabric-covered plastic headband, metal trim, or tin molding (what you might find around the base of a lamp or ceiling light fixture), or any flexible, strong material. Measure the base to fit around the top of the head.

1. Starting with a sturdy head-band, cover base completely with paper, ribbon, or other decorative material.

2. Cut paper into the desired crown pattern, such as scallops, graduated points, or a stylized triangle. Use a heavier decorative paper or mount thinner paper onto poster board.

3. Attach base to the crown using an adhesive appropriate for the materials chosen (see Adhesives in The Essentials section page 12).

4. Now for the fun part: Embellish at will with paper images, sequins, jewels, pom-pom trim, glitter, or what-ever your heart desires.

Wire Base Crown or Tiara

Wire is a crown-maker's best friend. It's easy to work with, extremely versatile, and offers a wonderfully delicate yet sturdy framework to showcase jewels and other embellishments. You can build a wire design as tall and ornate as you wish; use a heavier gauge wire for the base (16- or 18-gauge) and create a crown or tiara design with thinner wire (19- to 22-gauge). Thread your beads and crystals on 34-gauge wire.

Here we offer you the basic steps necessary for a standard wire frame:

1. Take a piece of 16- or 18-gauge (slightly less firm than a wire hanger) and cut to size with wire cutters. Bend it with your hands into a circular shape.

2. To make a fixed base, bring the ends together. Wrap a thinner wire around the two ends several times. Bend the ends of the thin wire back and pinch them together.

3. For an adjustable base, create a loop (or eye) on both ends with needle-nose pliers. Thread with ribbon.

4. Using a lighter gauge wire (between 19 and 22), begin your design. Wrap wire around base and build up, then bend it back down again. Continue until you've made a design you like.

5. Start attaching embellishments as you weave, such as beads, photos, and jewelry.

6. Wrap base with floral tape if desired, then wrap ribbon, fabric, or other flexible material on top of that.

7. To finish off wire, fold the end down and pinch it together with needle-nose pliers.

About the Authors

Kerri Judd

As long as I can remember, my interests have been every-thing artistic. Dolls, especially paper dolls that I colored and designed, ruled my childhood. While I should have been doing other things, I could only focus on making something pretty.

In high school, art classes were the only electives I ever took—no languages, just art. One year, I had three art classes back to back. Pure heaven. So now, although I couldn't speak my way out of a French paper bag, I can sure make it look great.

Of course, my greatest works of art are my children, Amy, Katie, and Nick. After years spent doodling and finger paint-ing with them, I am now enjoying a few grown-up projects once again, including business card design and painting murals. I have designed tags and nesting boxes for F.G. & Co. and designed a book on vintage shoes for the Memories of a Lifetime series (Sterling/Chapelle © 2004). My day job is spent working at the beautiful Paris to the Moon retail store in Costa Mesa, California.

My passion is collage. I love to make art tags, relishing the instant gratification because they are so small. I also mix my collage with other mediums, just for fun.

www.kerrijudd.com

Special thanks to Mom and Kim...you know why.

To Lowell for his incredible patience, love, and support. Amy, Katie, and Nick, my little jewels, you've been great.

Merci, Darren, you are a creative genius!

Thanks to Lisa for her glitter.

And to all of my friends who inspire me...I am blessed! I am surrounded by amazingly creative friends, some of whom are artists in this very book, sharing their talent for all to enjoy.

Danyel Montecinos

One of my earliest memories is watching my father stain a wall unit he made out of leftover kitchen cabinets. I grew up wearing extraordinary Halloween costumes that my mother made using things around the house. And don't even get me started on my brother Darren—he always tells me I could "make a silk purse out of a sow's ear" but he truly received an abundance of the family's artistic gene. He and I made wonderful things for our aunt's country store "way back when" and together we now operate Paris to the Moon in Costa Mesa, California.

My fifteen minutes of fame would have to be from my head confections that I call Maddie's Party Hats. It all started when my youngest daughter, then 4 years old, asked me to make her a party hat out of some embossed wallpaper. Impulsively, I began to add beautiful ribbons, vintage trims, and a few pieces of broken jewelry. My hats continue to evolve and change so they are always an exciting adventure.

My life as a mother of three—Kailey, Mason, and Madison—keeps me busy, but I still find time to show my work at many art shows throughout California and of course present the best of all possible hats, crowns, and tiaras for the princess within us all.

www.maddiescrownsandhats.com

Thank you to Guy Lotgering and Lora Ragole for all your help and infinite royal wisdom.

To Darren Calkins, for your cheerful abdication of Paris to the Moon during the photo shoot and for lending so many of your treasures for this book.

To Glenn, for your patience and support.

Contributing Artists

Ashley Carter
{queen of the follies}
pages 34,50,74,92,100

In Ashley Carter's world, details
are detailed. As the doyenne
of Goldbug Studio, Ashley
creates limited-edition and
one-of-a-kind collections of
sparkling handmade follies,
fairy tale-inspired figures, and decadent headpieces. A mixed
media artist with a background in textile design and mar-
keting, Ashley's first collection was introduced in 2001.

Each piece in the Goldbug Studio collection is created
in Raleigh, North Carolina; however, much inspiration is
derived from the artist's New Orleans roots. Creative freedom
means pairing the unexpected—fine family hand-me-downs,
1920s wallpaper, and Victorian oddities among them.

Goldbug Studio follies have been featured in *Modern Bride*,
Country Living, *Mary Engelbreit's Home Companion*, *Town & Country*,
Cottage Home, *Coast*, *Better Homes & Gardens*, *Southern Living Weddings*,
Romantic Homes, *Victorian Homes*, and *Southern Lady*. Ashley and
her team of talented assistants have created custom designs for
fabulous women, men, children, and pets around the globe.

Ashley lives in Raleigh, North Carolina with her husband,
Graham, and their super-hero cat, Syd.

www.goldbugstudio.com

Anna Corba
{queen of my studio}
pages 54,68,86

Anna Corba's journey into collage
began when her collections refused
to lay tame on her studio shelves.
Paper ephemera, found objects, and
ribbon began making their way into
her paintings, and as a way of sustain-
ing her newfound calling, she created a product line that
uses these materials in a functional yet whimsical manner.

Anna's journals, tags, candles, and cake pedestals can be
found in specialty stores across the country. She is the author
of *Vintage Paper Crafts* (Sterling/Chapelle © 2004) and *Making
Memory Boxes* (Sterling/Chapelle © 2005).

Anna lives with her sculptor husband in Northern
California and works out of her carriage house studio with
her dog, Caylus, at her feet.

www.annacorbastudio.com

Sandra Evertson
{queen of monkey business}

Sandra Evertson has been making things for as long as she can remember. She is a magpie collector of all things old, unique, and wonderful.

Sandra is truly a self-taught artist; her influences are many and varied, everything from "Charlie and the Chocolate Factory" and the glorious works of Faberge to "Dr. Seuss" and "Alice in Wonderland."

Perhaps that's why her pieces are always kind of off the beaten path. She likes to surround her workspace with all sorts of odds and ends, things that inspire her, that get the gears turning—funny little porcelain dolls, bits of mismatched jewelry, shiny whatnots, and lots of crumbly old books. For Sandra, it's very conducive to creating.

Sandra is the author of *Fanciful Paper Projects* (Sterling/Chapelle, © 2005) and *Fanciful Paper Flowers* (Sterling/Lark © 2007), and a regular contributor to *Romantic Homes* and Stampington & Company's array of artistic publications.

www.parisfleamarketdesigns.com

Pam Garrison
{queen of hunting & gathering}

Mixed media artist Pam Garrison is passionate about creating, having a need to "make things" ever since she first saw her mom sew, paint, and decorate handcrafted items. She also remembers seeing a favorite aunt's art space of her own, which was the definition of heaven to Pam. She realized that she had to make her dreams come true and set up a studio, where she could create to her heart's content.

Having finally honored her own artistic inclinations, Pam is passionate about inspiring others to do the same. She currently serves as a Director's Circle Artist for Stampington & Company and teaches both nationally and locally, and through it all she writes a blog about her adventures in trying to live a life full of creativity.

Pam lives in Southern California with her husband and two children. When not taking care of her family or playing in her studio she can often be found at flea markets, hunting and gathering vintage goodies to use in her vintage creations.

www.pamgarrison.com

Ulla Norup Milbrath
{queen of forgotten treasures and all things whimsical}

pages 32,82

Artist Ulla Norup Milbrath spent a truly gypsy-like childhood traveling the world. She studied design and art history in college and after graduating, she created and sold art dolls and jewelry for 15 years to clients such as the Smithsonian Museum.

Ulla taught high school art and ceramics for a few years and now teaches a variety of arts including paper and fiber arts, jewelry design, and paper-clay sculpting in her studio as well as at Castle In The Air in Berkeley, California.

Her artistic vision is rooted in memories, romance, and whimsy, with a heavy dose of love for nature and fantasy. Her happiest times have been those creating things with her own hands and then sharing them with others.

When not creating or teaching, Ulla loves to spend time chasing her dog, having picnics with her husband and daughter under the apple tree near her studio, and chatting online with her worldwide blog readers.

www.ullam.typepad.com

Nicol Sayre
{queen of playing with dolls}

pages 76,94

Nicol Sayre's world is filled with hoopskirts and flounces, tiaras and top hats, tinsel and glitter. With wonderful antique fabrics and dolls and vintage playthings as her inspiration, Nicol creates one-of-a-kind and limited-edition dolls, paper dolls, and whimsical characters. Her creations are simple yet elegant and steeped in tradition but always with an underlying sense of playfulness and just a bit of quirkiness.

Her mother taught Nicol to sew and she spent her childhood drawing little pictures of fancy dresses and playing "fabric store." Nicol has designed patterns and collectibles, but her true love is making original dolls for which she has an incredible following of wonderfully loyal customers. A glimpse of her art and home have appeared in *Mary Engelbreit's Home Companion, Country Living, Country Home,* and *Better Homes & Gardens,* as well as several books.

Nicol creates at home in Northern California with her husband and two daughters and a silly dog named Lily.

www.nicolsayre.com

Barbara Schriber
{queen of chaos}

page 70

Barbara Schriber used her move from California to Idaho in 2002 as an opportunity for a career change. With encouragement from her husband, Scott, and artistic provisions from her mother, Melissa Neufeld, Barbara quit her finance job and started handcrafting paper gifts. Unable to draw, paint, or sculpt, Barbara never thought of herself as artistic.

Initially she struggled with the creative process, but her mom's expression to "just start something and see where it takes you" persuaded her to take a chance. Barbara now encourages other women to find their own artist within.

As hard as she tries to be organized, Barbara is always amid a messy car, desk, barn, or studio. Ironically, that is when she achieves the most.

www.barbaraschriberdesigns.com

Denise Sharp
{queen of gleam}

pages 46,98

Denise Sharp, the proprietor of Studio d. Sharp, is a visual artist with a fine arts degree in sculpture and printmaking from California College of the Arts. Denise is an avid collector and her house and studio swell with vintage ephemera and quirky collections that serve to inspire.

While most businesses start with a business plan, Denise started with a birthday party. After making elaborate paper hats for all of the guests at her son's first birthday party, she began to receive orders for more. Her body of work is derived from her reverence for vintage charm and her desire to imbue her own celebrations with extraordinary details.

D. Sharp products are sold in more than 100 specialty boutiques across the country. Her work has appeared in *Country Home, Mary Engelbreit's Home Companion, InStyle,* and *Martha Stewart Weddings.* More importantly, innumerable brides, gift-givers, and celebrants have chosen Denise's work to be a special part of their own memorable occasions.

Denise lives in her hometown of Portland, Oregon with her husband, Gil, and their two sons, Mason and Calder.

www.studiodsharp.com

Dianne Stickley White
{queen of the macabre}

page 112

Dianne has always had a fondness for Halloween. As a child she didn't own a teddy bear; she did, however, have a rubber skeleton.

Halloween being her favorite holiday, festivities were planned out weeks in advance. Papier-mâché zombie heads, corpse brides, and huge spiders with even bigger webs were just a few projects she and her sister used to make their house the scariest on the block.

Dianne even incorporated the macabre into her wedding plans. Not only did she plan an October wedding, but also a haunted masquerade ball for the reception. Gravestones and bride-and-groom skeletons decorated the reception hall, as friends and family arrived wearing their spookiest costumes.

"Being 'Queen of the Macabre' is just doing what I love and being me," says Dianne.

www.petalsandgreenscottage.com

Metric Equivalency Charts

mm-millimeters cm-centimeters
inches to millimeters and centimeters

inches	mm	cm	inches	cm	inches	cm
1/8	3	0.3	9	22.9	30	76.2
1/4	6	0.6	10	25.4	31	78.7
1/2	13	1.3	12	30.5	33	83.8
5/8	16	1.6	13	33.0	34	86.4
3/4	19	1.9	14	35.6	35	88.9
7/8	22	2.2	15	38.1	36	91.4
1	25	2.5	16	40.6	37	94.0
1 1/4	32	3.2	17	43.2	38	96.5
1 1/2	38	3.8	18	45.7	39	99.1
1 3/4	44	4.4	19	48.3	40	101.6
2	51	5.1	20	50.8	41	104.1
2 1/2	64	6.4	21	53.3	42	106.7
3	76	7.6	22	55.9	43	109.2
3 1/2	89	8.9	23	58.4	44	111.8
4	102	10.2	24	61.0	45	114.3
4 1/2	114	11.4	25	63.5	46	116.8
5	127	12.7	26	66.0	47	119.4
6	152	15.2	27	68.6	48	121.9
7	178	17.8	28	71.1	49	124.5
8	203	20.3	29	73.7	50	127.0

yards to meters

yards	meters	yards	meters	yards	meters	yards	meters	yards	meters
1/8	0.11	2 1/8	1.94	4 1/8	3.77	6 1/8	5.60	8 1/8	7.43
1/4	0.23	2 1/4	2.06	4 1/4	3.89	6 1/4	5.72	8 1/4	7.54
3/8	0.34	2 3/8	2.17	4 3/8	4.00	6 3/8	5.83	8 3/8	7.66
1/2	0.46	2 1/2	2.29	4 1/2	4.11	6 1/2	5.94	8 1/2	7.77
5/8	0.57	2 5/8	2.40	4 5/8	4.23	6 5/8	6.06	8 5/8	7.89
3/4	0.69	2 3/4	2.51	4 3/4	4.34	6 3/4	6.17	8 3/4	8.00
7/8	0.80	2 7/8	2.63	4 7/8	4.46	6 7/8	6.29	8 7/8	8.12
1	0.91	3	2.74	5	4.57	7	6.40	9	8.23
1 1/8	1.03	3 1/8	2.86	5 1/8	4.69	7 1/8	6.52	9 1/8	8.34
1 1/4	1.14	3 1/4	2.97	5 1/4	4.80	7 1/4	6.63	9 1/4	8.46
1 3/8	1.26	3 3/8	3.09	5 3/8	4.91	7 3/8	6.74	9 3/8	8.57
1 1/2	1.37	3 1/2	3.20	5 1/2	5.03	7 1/2	6.86	9 1/2	8.69
1 5/8	1.49	3 5/8	3.31	5 5/8	5.14	7 5/8	6.97	9 5/8	8.80
1 3/4	1.60	3 3/4	3.43	5 3/4	5.26	7 3/4	7.09	9 3/4	8.92
1 7/8	1.71	3 7/8	3.54	5 7/8	5.37	7 7/8	7.20	9 7/8	9.03
2	1.83	4	3.66	6	5.49	8	7.32	10	9.14

Index